Praise for *Overcoming Your Difficult Family*

"With gentle humor and compassion, Eric Maisel acts as a wise friend in this clear and practical guide that offers specific tools for navigating the roughest of family seas. It even helps you calm the waters! A wonderfully useful, unique, and comforting book."
— **Judith Schlesinger, PhD**, author of *The Insanity Hoax*

"Eric Maisel rejects diagnostic labels in this insightful, practical, and extremely helpful book. Anyone should find his no-nonsense approach and practical tips useful."
— **James B. Gottstein, Esq.**,
President of the Law Project for Psychiatric Rights

"Throughout this book, Dr. Maisel maintains a nonmedical and nonpathology theme, describing family problems as natural human phenomena rather than mental disorders. His eight skills are introduced and applied step-by-step within the context of several unique family cultures whose members unwittingly develop problematic ways of coping. This refreshing guide to overcoming interpersonal conflict with respect for personal diversity, coexistence, and cooperation is invigorating to those of us who struggle to rehumanize the mental health industry!"
— **Chuck Ruby, PhD**, executive director of the
International Society for Ethical Psychology and Psychiatry

"With characteristic clarity, Dr. Eric Maisel lays out an approach to family difficulties that cuts through the surface tension to reach the compassionate core of human relationships. An accessible guide grounded in current research and the author's own clinical experience."
— **Dr. Dale McGowan**, coauthor of *Raising Freethinkers*

"Dr. Maisel offers more than just understanding; he also offers hope by way of practical suggestions for dealing with difficult family members that can provide relief for those who have for years been beleaguered by hard-to-deal-with parents, siblings, in-laws, and others. I recommend this book not only to family, individual, and couples therapists but also to the clients with whom they work."
— **James E. Maddux, PhD**, George Mason University
Professor Emeritus, Department of Psychology

"*Overcoming Your Difficult Family* is a treasure trove of ideas and strategies. Eric Maisel has a gift for making complicated ideas easy to understand. I'm sure anyone who is struggling with family relationships of any sort will find something in this book that they can identify with and that's bound to help them!"

— **Sami Timimi**, Consultant Child and Adolescent Psychiatrist,
Director of Medical Education,
Lincolnshire Partnership Foundation NHS Trust

"This may be the most important book you will ever read. If you want to have a more joyful life and a relationship full of real, lasting love, this book is for you. Practical and powerful, it will teach you how to be smart, strong, calm, clear, aware, brave, present, and resilient — qualities that too many of us lack living in our stressed-out world. Get a copy for yourself and one for everyone in your family. It will change your life."

— **Jed Diamond, PhD**, author of *The Enlightened Marriage*

"This accessible book shines a liberating light on past family pain and patterns as it offers new skills and hope for creating the healthy, supportive family you've always dreamed of — right here, right now. Highly recommended!"

— **Donald Altman, LPC**, bestselling author of
The Mindfulness Toolbox and *One-Minute Mindfulness*

"Spoiler alert: after you read *Overcoming Your Difficult Family*, you will feel less distress and be more able to utilize your personal power to create the life you want! Dr. Maisel eloquently offers practical tools on every page, teaching you how to stay calm and effective in even the most challenging family environment. You will be equipped with the knowledge of what family type you are from, and you will learn eight essential skills to overcome lingering family-of-origin problems that have, consciously or unconsciously, caused you upset for years. In short, this book will set you free."

— **Dr. Lee Jampolsky**, author of *Healing the Addictive Personality*
and founder of Inspirational Psychology

"An uber-pragmatic how-to guide on overcoming not just your difficult family but your own internal demons. Through powerful examples, exercises, and tips, Maisel masterfully guides you to cultivate eight pillars of inner strength. Thoughtful, empowering, and practical, this book will help you overcome whatever family pattern may still be holding you back in your life and your relationships!"

— **Anna Yusim, MD**, psychiatrist and author of *Fulfilled*

OVERCOMING YOUR DIFFICULT FAMILY

Also by Eric Maisel

OVERCOMING YOUR DIFFICULT FAMILY

8 Skills for Thriving in Any Family Situation

ERIC MAISEL, PhD

New World Library
Novato, California

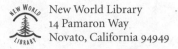

New World Library
14 Pamaron Way
Novato, California 94949

Text design by Tona Pearce Myers

Library of Congress Cataloging-in-Publication Data
Names: Maisel, Eric, [date]–author.
Title: Overcoming your difficult family : 8 skills for thriving in any family
    situation / Eric Maisel.
Description: Novato, CA : New World Library, 2017. | Includes bibliographical
    references and index.
Identifiers: LCCN 2016059697 (print) | LCCN 2017014046 (ebook) | ISBN
    9781608684526 (Ebook) | ISBN 9781608684519 (paperback)
Subjects: LCSH: Self-actualization (Psychology) | Communication in families.
    | Family psychotherapy. | BISAC: SELF-HELP / Personal Growth / General.
    | PSYCHOLOGY / Psychotherapy / Couples & Family. | FAMILY & RELA-
    TIONSHIPS / Conflict Resolution.
Classification: LCC BF637.S4 (ebook) | LCC BF637.S4 M3345 2017 (print) | DDC
    158.2/4—dc23
LC record available at https://lccn.loc.gov/2016059697

First printing, June 2017
ISBN 978-1-60868-451-9
Ebook ISBN 978-1-60868-452-6

Printed in Canada on 100% postconsumer-waste recycled paper

New World Library is proud to be a Gold Certified Environmentally Responsible Publisher. Publisher certification awarded by Green Press Initiative. www.greenpressinitiative.org

10   9   8   7   6   5   4   3   2   1

For Ann, as always

And for Ethan, Abigail, and Elise

Contents

Introduction

There is no pill that can make family life easy. There is no pill that can spare you pain if one of your parents is alcoholic, one of your children is troubled, or your mate is cheating on you. M. Scott Peck begins *The Road Less Traveled* with a simple, eloquent announcement: "Life is difficult." Tolstoy famously begins *Anna Karenina* in an equally eloquent way: "All happy families are alike; each unhappy family is unhappy in its own way." Working as a family therapist with families and couples, as a life coach and creativity coach with individuals, and as a mental health reformer within a system that isn't helpful enough, I know that family life regularly takes its toll and that when it does, useful help can be hard to find.

In *Overcoming Your Difficult Family* I present eight skills that you can employ to survive difficult family life and sometimes even improve it for everyone involved. I also describe ten different sorts of difficult families — variously troubled by sadness and anxiety, bullying and abuse, a lack of love and too much emotional distance, and so on. I explain how you can employ the eight skills in each of these difficult family situations.

Part of what makes family life so difficult sometimes is that it's hard to avoid. Because of the intimacy and interconnectedness of family living, each person is held hostage to the personalities, agendas, and shadows of everyone else. You can't easily avoid your mother or your father, your mate, your children, or your siblings. In a picture-postcard family, where everyone loves one another, roots for one another, and never criticizes anyone else, every family member may flourish. In many families, people may be struggling just to survive.

In this book you'll learn how to stay calm even in a highly stressful environment, how to maintain your balance in the middle of family crises, how to set boundaries that keep you safe and sane, and more. No matter how you personally experience emotional distress in your family life — as anxiety, despair, addiction, procrastination, mental confusion, or physical symptoms, for example — I'll help you acquire the tools you need to make every day feel at least a little better.

~~~~~~

TIP: You may be accustomed to thinking of your "symptoms," like feeling nervous, sad, or distracted, as "personal" problems. But they may be family problems, including lingering family-of-origin problems. Families can be toxic and can cause inner disturbances. You may find your "personal" problems dramatically reduced when you overcome your present or past difficult family!

~~~~~~

Family difficulties take many forms. One of your parents may be alcoholic, abusive, and unreliable. Your mate may be absent, distant, and barely there for you. Your teenage child may be having school difficulties. Your older sister or brother may be scathing and cruel. Sometimes these difficulties are subtle and hard to grasp: you don't really feel happy or safe inside your family, but you can't quite put your finger on what makes it feel dangerous.

Any grouping of human beings produces difficulties because each member of the group has his or her own personality, opinions, agendas, defensive style, mood swings, and habitual ways of being indifferent to and careless about the needs of others. All of this is intensified in a family, where you may be expected to rely on family members who may not be reliable, care for family members for whom you don't feel real affection, and deal constantly with family members who may be hard — or even impossible — to interact with.

The eight skills I present here are things you can start doing right away. You don't have to wait for anyone else in your family to change. Maybe some of them will be influenced to make changes by the work that you do on yourself and for yourself, but you can't control their choices. All you can do is take charge of you.

It is very common nowadays for an unwanted feeling, such as sadness, or an unwanted behavior, like a child's restlessness at school, to be identified as a symptom of a mental disorder and for the person who experiences or exhibits it to be labeled as a person with a mental disorder. I do not believe in this paradigm or in this labeling system. In this book, I consciously use the word *sadness* (and related words like *despair* and *unhappiness*) rather than the word *depression*. It is likely that those feelings and behaviors are the natural consequences of a person's life experiences, including the experience of growing up in a difficult family. This is likely true even if someone experiences unusual symptoms, such as auditory or visual hallucinations. Such symptoms, feelings, and behaviors are rather more likely caused by some persistent early trauma, like growing up in a toxic family, than by the sorts of biological or chemical malfunctions that are usually characterized as mental illness.

Most mental health professionals subscribe to the current paradigm that classifies depression as a diagnosable disorder that is best treated with chemical interventions, called *psychiatric medication*, and with expert talk, called *psychotherapy*. A smaller but sizable number of mental health professionals assert that there is no scientific evidence for this paradigm, that mental-disorder diagnoses are labels affixed to phenomena primarily for the sake of making money, and that the current paradigm is misguided at best and fraudulent at worst. Because I'm in this second camp, I intend to use ordinary language throughout this book and speak about sadness, rather than clinical depression or bipolar disorder; about anxiety, rather than generalized anxiety disorder; about compulsions rather than obsessive-compulsive disorder; and so on.

If you want to learn more about my point of view on this issue, which is shared by other practitioners in a movement that is variously called critical psychology, critical psychiatry, or antipsychiatry, please see my book *The Future of Mental Health* or consult the reading list on my website www.thefuture ofmentalhealth.com.

It is completely reasonable and realistic to expect that toxic families cause harm to family members and produce, or at least contribute to, results like sadness, anxiety, and addiction. It seems unlikely, however, that there are straightforward or causal connections between being exposed to a difficult family situation and experiencing specific "mental disorder symptoms" or emotional challenges. The fact that you grew up in an anxious family, say, doesn't mean that you will necessarily manifest the symptoms of "generalized anxiety disorder," and having to deal with addicted family members does not mean that you will inevitably succumb to an addiction. But it seems reasonable to speculate that being bullied, abused, or treated aggressively might result in symptoms like nightmares, which are commonly seen as signs of "post-traumatic stress disorder." It seems logical that if you grew up in a strict, rule-bound family, you might become burdened by obsessive-compulsive symptoms. The purpose of such speculating is not to draw causal connections but rather to help you think about your own suffering in a different way. You might begin to say to yourself, "Oh, these are some of the natural consequences of having grown up in my particular toxic environment," rather than concluding, "I have a mental disorder." Then you could begin to apply your new skill set to the task of dealing with those natural but unfortunate consequences.

There are many approaches you might take in this effort, from engaging in family therapy to entering recovery (if addiction is an issue) to getting a better grip on your mind (and the thoughts that pester and plague you) through a mindfulness practice. Mastering the eight skills I describe will give you a significantly better chance of reducing your experience of emotional distress and surviving your difficult family.

The eight skills — or qualities, or attributes — are *smarts, strength, calmness, clarity, awareness, courage, presence,* and *resilience.* You already have a commonsense understanding of the nature and value of these skills; now I would love to have you think of them as an actual skill set or tool kit that you can employ in any family situation — and anywhere else in your life, for that matter — to help you feel less distress, increase your personal power, and live the life that you want.

I also suggest some ceremonies to try to give you stronger ownership of the skills. By *ceremony* I mean an activity carried out for a particular purpose and performed in a ritualized or formalized way. It might be anything from lighting a candle to breathing and thinking in a certain way to a much more elaborate sequence of actions, words, and thoughts. Important ceremonies in life, like exchanging wedding vows or raising your hand in a citizenship ceremony, are powerful. beautiful, and important experiences. Creating your own ceremonies to celebrate your skills and growth may make your family life feel less difficult.

After describing each skill, I show how you can use the skills in your particular situation. Toward that end I've created ten categories of difficult families, not because I believe that problem families come neatly packaged and labeled but to help us think about the concrete and different challenges that arise.

Of course, multiple problems can arise within a single family. Maybe your mother was sad and anxious, your father was compulsive and addicted to alcohol, one of your brothers was bullying and aggressive, and another of your brothers was rule-bound and punitive. There are all sorts of combinations and permutations possible — and it's likely that your situation is some perplexing, idiosyncratic blend of these characteristic types.

Dianne's Story

Here's how Dianne, a client of mine, explained the situations in her family of origin and in her current family:

> I grew up with a sad and anxious mother and a dramatic and chaotic father. As a result, it was difficult for me to figure out what kind of world it was. Sometimes my mother's energy dominated, and we all seemed bathed in depression; sometimes my father's chaotic energy caused violent upheavals. Eventually my father abandoned our family, which plunged my mother deeper into depression.
>
> I was responsible for holding everything together in the family, without much assistance from my family or from anyone else. Therefore, as I came out of childhood, I thought I wanted rules. This probably pushed me to select a spouse from a rule-bound and punitive family, someone who was also intrusive and overvigilant. For some time, his rules were tolerable and the emotional distance not too drastic, and I made do. But of course, over time life felt worse and worse.
>
> I've found that, while I'm still very uncertain about what's reasonable and not reasonable in relationships, because of the uncertainty of my childhood, I do have a few clear ideas nowadays. I know that rules alone do not suffice to create a human experience. I know that closeness is necessary and that its absence feels horrible. I have become increasingly frustrated over the years

about being in what has proved to be a loveless and distant relationship.

Understanding where all this may have come from is not as helpful to me as knowing what to do about it now. Now I must be willing to rock the boat and risk the potential upheaval. I need to manifest the skills you've described, strength and courage being the first among them. Maybe making those changes will influence the situation, maybe they won't, but I can't expect anything good to happen if I refuse to step up to the plate!

Families are complicated — and so are people!

Your Eight-Skills Tool Kit

Throughout this book I use the metaphor of a tool kit, inviting you to build and stock it with your eight skills. I think this metaphor is helpful because it gives us a concrete image of solving a problem. Just as a mechanic selects the right size and shape of wrench to adjust a bolt, if you visualize yourself as always carrying a tool kit stocked with powerful, useful tools, then, when a family situation erupts or is about to erupt, you can take a step back, open your tool kit (maybe literally, for example by pulling out a sheet of paper on which you've listed these eight skills), and ask yourself, "Which tools do I need right now?" If you're being bullied, you might need strength and courage. When your child is having a meltdown, you might need presence and awareness. When you and your mate seem to be engaged in the same conflict for the umpteenth time, you might need to employ your smarts and calmness. By understanding that you have these skills always available to you and by reminding yourself that different situations call for different responses, you put yourself in the best position possible to handle the particular difficulty confronting you.

Whatever your family situation and whatever blends of toxicity you've been obliged to deal with, your most helpful response is to manifest the eight skills I'm about to describe. Let's begin!

PART ONE

Your Family
Survival Tool Kit

CHAPTER ONE

Being Smart

The first step in taking charge of your life and better surviving your difficult family is to be smart. I don't mean being book smart or big-brain smart. I mean being aware, insightful, savvy, and strategic. Often the smartest writer isn't the most successful writer, and the smartest scientist isn't the one making the breakthrough discoveries. Likewise, often the smartest child in class is also the most troubled child, and the smartest college student is the one who drops out of college. It doesn't matter how much native intelligence you have if you aren't also insightful, alert, and aware.

You want to be smart about what's actually going on around you — in life and particularly in your family. This is much harder to do than it sounds. It isn't easy to know how to think about life, your circumstances, or what is actually causing your difficulties. If, for example, you are sad, you may presume or be told that you have the mental disorder of depression. However, it may be your family life, your work life, your school life, or your relationship that is making you feel hopeless and despairing. There is a big difference between having a mental disorder and hating work, hating school, or having a miserable time in your family. If we incorrectly identify what is going on, we set ourselves off in what may prove a fruitless, counterproductive, and even dangerous direction.

Be smart about what's going on by asking the simple but profound question, "What is really going on in my life that is making it feel so difficult?" Be patient as you try to answer it. We usually race through life and rarely stop to think quietly. As a starting point, you might brainstorm a list of possible causes. It might sound like this: "I know I'm feeling sad. What's really causing my sadness? It might be the way Bob's treating me. If it's that, I have to look that in the eye. It might be that work is such a grind. It might be that I haven't realized any of my dreams. It may be how ungrateful our children are acting — and how rude they are! If it's any of those things, I have to look it in the eye."

Likewise, you want to be smart and honest about your part in whatever is going on. You want to be smart about identifying things you can't control, things you might be able to influence, and things you can't influence. You want to be smart about your everyday survival and safety: Yes, it may prove a tremendous financial hardship to leave your abusive husband, but how smart is it to allow yourself to be hurt? You want to be smart about your methods: Does yelling at your children get you the results you're after? Maybe it feels good for a moment to let your anger and disappointment out that way — but is it smart?

Take the situation of my client Maureen, a writer. Without quite realizing it, she found herself being held hostage by her husband's so-called clinical depression. She could work on her novel only when her husband wasn't too down. Whenever she got on a roll with her writing, he seemed to take a nosedive, often to the point of threatening suicide. As obvious as this dynamic was to anyone looking at it from the outside, it nevertheless took Maureen several coaching sessions to really understand how she was being held hostage by her husband's moods.

I asked Maureen, "What would be smart for you to do, given this dynamic?" She instantly replied, "Getting away on some days and writing in a café."

I could sense her hesitation. "And?" I asked.

"If I was away writing and he harmed himself, I really couldn't take that," she replied.

We began working on helping her inch her way toward actually doing what she knew she ought to do — go out and write — even though the idea provoked strong feelings of guilt and dread.

She knew what would be smart for her to do — but she could also tell how dangerous it would feel to actually do it, and she had to call on her courage as well as her smarts. We typically need to manifest all eight skills to counter the negative effects of our difficult family.

Finally Maureen managed to leave the house to write. Instead of worsening, as she feared that it would, her situation improved. It turned out that hovering over her semi-invalid husband and keeping a constant watch on him was not what he needed from her. Just as she had needed air, he needed some too. One day she came home to discover that he had done the laundry. This might not sound like much, but when you are living inside a difficult family, the markers by which we see improvement and change are often small markers like the unexpected blessing of clean clothes.

CEREMONY: Taking Time to Reflect

At least once a day, find a quiet, private place, get yourself comfortably seated and settled, shut your eyes, and take a few deep, cleansing breaths. Remind yourself that you pride yourself on being an alert, aware, savvy human being, and gently ask yourself, "Am I being smart about what's bothering me?"

Take your time, and give yourself a chance to think and feel through your situation and arrive at some useful answers. If nothing is bothering you on a given day, then enact a small ceremony of celebration instead!

One way to get smarter about family life is getting a handle on what sort of family you live in. Do you live in a family where everything is a drama? Do you live among anxious people who make you anxious? Are you part of a family in which love is in short supply? What dynamics characterize your family life? For example, is your family made up of cliques that are at war with one another? In part 2, when we look at different family types, I encourage you to ask yourself, "What would be smart for me to start doing in order to survive my sort of difficult family?"

Being smart in the context of difficult family life can mean a variety of things: avoiding a given family member, speaking up and saying what needs to be said, changing your attitude and opting to be less critical or more loving, aiming for more closeness or more distance, changing your part in the dynamic between you and other family members, or getting clearer about your life purposes and separating from your family's dramas.

~~~~~~

Tip: Be Specific

Is there one specific problem making your family life difficult? It might be money troubles: not being able to pay your bills, not having medical insurance, or having to live from paycheck to paycheck. It might be the special needs of a family member: a parent with dementia or a child with a chronic disability. It might be issues of trust and betrayal: a philandering mate, an untrustworthy adolescent child, or a regularly disappearing parent. Take a moment to see if there is anything new to be learned when you ask yourself: "Is there something smart I might try to help me deal with this problem?"

~~~~~~

Think of some words that are synonyms for smart — *savvy, clever, strategic, sharp, astute, cagey, shrewd, streetwise.* What they all share is an attitude: I'm not going to be defeated! Right now the difficulties that burden you may seem as though they arise from your personal failings, but they may in fact be rooted in family and interpersonal dynamics. Whether they are personal or interpersonal, they may be weighing so heavily on you that it is hard for you to feel sharp, astute, or clever.

Please announce that you do not want to stand defeated, that you do not want to live a life of constant sadness, that you want instead to vote for life and to come out of the shadows. When you do, you will put yourself in a position to be smart about what's going on, smart about protecting yourself better, smart about making needed changes. Start there, by standing up, coming out of the shadows, and enlisting your smarts in the service of a vastly improved life!

Adding Smarts to Your Tool Kit

1. What would help you get smarter, in the sense I've described above?

2. Imagine that you had an actual tool kit with tools in it. Spend a little time visualizing your "smart" tool. What might it look like? How might you use it? In your mind's eye, practice taking it out of your tool kit and using it.

3. Do you contribute to your family difficulties? If so, in what ways? Be smart about bravely examining that question, starting now.

4. In what areas of your family life or your personal life do you think it might pay you to be smarter? Try to be specific.

CHAPTER TWO

Being Strong

Living in a difficult family requires fortitude, stamina, and strength. Being criticized over and over again is more wearing and more tiring than a long march; feeling abandoned, misunderstood, or rejected is harder on the system than climbing a mountain.

We need great strength in order to say what we mean, if that feels threatening and comes with a history of retaliation. We need great strength to stay present through our teenager's tantrums and rebellions. We need great strength to deal with a mate who envies our success, a parent who snickers at our life choices, or a child who requires our constant attention. Family life is nothing if not demanding.

CEREMONY: Acknowledging Strength

Often we live as a weakened version of ourselves because life has beaten us down, because we've failed too many times and no longer trust ourselves to succeed, because we have trouble holding a clear vision of our life purposes and our most important intentions, or for other reasons.

If you are living a weakened version of yourself, you might want to create and enact a ceremony to strengthen yourself. For example, find or create a symbol of strength: maybe a tiger, a tree bent by a constant wind that is still sturdy and strong, or something gentle but powerful, such as a flower or a child's smile. Find or create your personal symbol, have it made into a piece of jewelry, wear it, and then ceremonially touch it regularly during the day, saying or thinking, "I am strong" or some other phrase that reminds you to live powerfully.

Living in a difficult family can weaken you tremendously. You will need to muster and manifest your strength right in the middle of those difficult circumstances — when your mother is threatening to disown you, your husband is snickering at you, or your son is throwing a teenage-size tantrum. Carve out time and space, create and enact a ceremony of strength, and begin the process of living strongly.

This is not the kind of strength we can acquire in the gym (though being healthy and fit can be helpful too): it is an internal fortitude that we must muster and manifest. Being strong means instantly silencing self-talk like "I can't do that" with a firm "Yes, I can!" When I work with clients, we often spend a lot of time focusing on mustering and manifesting strength.

Sometimes it requires rehearsing what you intend to say and visualizing the interaction in all its details, including the possibly negative consequences.

One of my clients hated the fact that her husband would not follow through on a "simple" household project. Their downstairs bathroom needed a new toilet, and her husband had gotten as far as removing the old toilet and placing it in a corner of their living room. That old toilet had sat there for months! Not only was it an eyesore that prevented her from socializing in her own home, but to her it represented living proof of the difficulties she was having in her marriage and a living reproach that screamed at her, "You are so weak!"

It took all her strength to give her husband the ultimatum that the toilet in the living room was a marriage deal-breaker. Even with that ultimatum, he took his sweet time finishing the remodel — but at least the day came when the old toilet finally left the living room.

Another client found that she was being held hostage by her mother's last will and testament. She had devoted her life to caring for her aged mother. Each time she tried to suggest that some other arrangement might be made so that she, the daughter, could have a life, the mother would threaten to remove her from her will. This threat had worked for many years.

It took us some sessions to discern what concrete strength she needed to muster to free herself from the grip of that dangled legacy. Finally we figured out that she needed to buy a plane ticket to the place where she had long dreamed of relocating, with an eye to scouting it out. With that ticket in hand, she was finally strong enough to have the conversation with her mother that she had needed to have for so long — no matter what her mother threatened about bequests.

A third client needed to find the strength to continue with her writing even though her husband had grown very envious of her success. She came to me not understanding why she wasn't writing, given that she loved writing, felt connected to her current writing project, had readers waiting for it, and could sense no earthly reason why she wasn't writing. She noted that her husband craved the income she brought in but also belittled her efforts. It quickly became clear that his resentment of her success had somehow crept into her psyche and caused her to block her own efforts to write.

To overcome this block, the strength she had to muster was the strength to live with a passive-aggressive mate. She had to tune him out, call him on his behaviors (like filling up her writing study with "things we don't have room for in the garage"), and speak to him clearly and directly about not belittling her readers, her genre of writing, or her efforts.

A fourth client had to find the strength to send her teenager away to a therapeutic wilderness camp despite his loud objections. For several years he'd been doing progressively worse in school, picking up a drug and alcohol habit, and finally dealing drugs. Even being caught and facing prosecution did not seem to wake her son up to his predicament.

My client saw this wilderness camp as her last hope, and she had to muster all her strength to demand that he go, over his violent protestations and threats of self-harm. In fact, the wilderness-camp experience seemed to turn his life around. This is often the sort of blessing a person receives when she is able to manifest strength within a troubled or difficult family.

~~~~~~

Tips for Increasing Your Strength

Wear Armor. You can't wear a literal suit of armor, but you *can* grow a thicker skin. You can toughen your hide by deciding that you reject the right of a family member to criticize you; by accepting in a deep way that everyone has an opinion and that the only opinion about you that matters is yours; by not giving in when someone in your family importunes you in their characteristic way; and by not growing defensive when someone makes a snide or damning remark about you. Families are full of carelessly flung arrows, pointed darts, and countless pinpricks. Your new thicker skin is your first line of defense against all that family sharpness!

Try the following guided visualization or one like it: *Close your eyes. Picture your skin as thicker and tougher than it is right now. Picture it as tough as a rhinoceros's hide or the skin of a superhero. Now picture a family member whose words regularly hurt you. Picture that person's words as arrows flying in your direction. Don't flinch. Feel them bounce painlessly off your thick, tough hide. Watch your family member turn away in frustration!*

Train Your Warrior's Mind. A warrior trains his mind as well as his body. He is resolute about thinking only thoughts that serve him. A thought about the best tactics for victory serves him; a thought that overestimates his opponent's strength or overdramatizes the danger he faces does not.

He tries to be clear and accurate in his thinking so that he can make realistic plans and execute them effectively. If he must wait for days to execute an ambush, he must not let his mind play tricks on him and weaken him as he waits. You have the same job: to get an iron grip on your mind. That iron grip is the greatest strength you possess.

Say the phrase "I am strong" one hundred times today. Keep a count. Don't be embarrassed by saying those words so many times. You want the idea to really take hold. Say the phrase all through your daily life, while you're stalled in traffic, while you're shopping for groceries, in situations that call for strength as well as in situations that don't particularly. Make a point of saying it if you are feeling weak. At such times it isn't a lie but a wish: the wish to actually be strong in all situations!

~~~~~~

You might also try to increase your physical strength by getting in better shape; increase your existential strength by articulating your values, principles, and life purposes; hone your tactical skills by learning to make plans and rehearse interactions; increase your vocal strength by practicing a little private roaring; increase your endurance by setting yourself tasks and goals just a little out of your reach or your comfort zone and then accomplishing them; and by dreaming up other ways of making yourself a stronger person every day.

Strength is primarily a mindset. It is you saying "I am the hero of my story," "I am a powerful, valuable person who matters," and "I approach life from a place of strength and not weakness." It is nothing like arrogance, grandiosity, or narcissism, though of course it can veer or incline in those directions. Rather, it is you standing up. Especially if you grew up in a difficult family where standing up for yourself was routinely and severely punished, this may not be easy for you. Gain that skill by practicing it: remind yourself that you want to be your strongest self, and prime yourself to manifest your strength in real-life situations.

Adding Strength to Your Tool Kit

1. What in your current family situation weakens you? Try to be clear and specific.
2. Name some ways that you would like to grow stronger. Identify the steps you mean to take in order to get stronger in those ways.

CHAPTER THREE

Being Calm

It is hard for people to achieve regular rather than intermittent calmness. All human beings experience anxiety. We have a brain that naturally races, and many people experience life-long agitation as a result of early adverse experiences. Because anxiety is a feature of the human condition and because life in a difficult family increases that anxiety, the skill of calmness may currently be eluding you.

You're probably aware of the role that anxiety plays in your difficulties with calmness, and you may also be aware of the fact that early trauma, if you had to endure it, has made you more anxious than the next person. But you may not be aware that your brain is built to look out for — and obsess about — potential threats, and that it never really stops doing that vigilant appraising, even while we sleep or try to sleep. Our racing brain interferes with our ability to maintain calmness. Between that and our natural anxiety, it's hard to ever feel very settled!

The challenges of living agitate us, distract us, and unsettle us; and our pestering, unproductive thoughts rattle us. Even if we do manage to attain calmness in one part of our life — say, during our meditation practice or while walking in nature — that calmness may vanish as soon as we step into our family circle and start dealing with the problems that make family life so difficult. Calmness is hard to attain, and it is hardest to attain when we need it the most.

Fortunately, there are many strategies and techniques that can help us achieve and maintain a satisfactory level of calmness, including breathing techniques, relaxation techniques, cognitive techniques, detachment techniques, reorienting techniques, mindfulness techniques, and discharge techniques.

~~~~~~

Ten Tips for Anxiety Management

Here are ten anxiety-management techniques that are well worth trying. Please practice all of these to discern which ones work best for you.

- *Deep breathing.* The simplest — and a very powerful — anxiety management technique is deep breathing. By breathing slowly and deeply (five seconds on the inhale, five seconds on the exhale), you stop your racing mind and alert your body to the fact that you wish to be calmer.
- *Cognitive self-help.* Changing the way you think is a powerful antianxiety strategy. You can do this straightforwardly by (1) noticing what you are saying to yourself; (2) disputing the self-talk that makes you anxious or that does not serve you; and (3) substituting more

affirmative, calming, or useful self-talk. This three-step process really works.

- *Incantation.* A variation on the two strategies above is to use them together by accompanying your deep breaths with a useful thought, thinking half the thought on the inhale and the second half on the exhale. Incantations that might reduce your experience of anxiety include "I am perfectly calm" and "I can thrive in my family." Experiment with some short phrases and find one or two that serve to calm you.

- *Physical relaxation techniques.* Physical relaxation techniques range from simple procedures, such as rubbing your shoulder, to more elaborate "progressive relaxation techniques," in which you slowly relax each part of your body in turn. Doing something physically soothing can be really effective in helping you calm yourself.

- *Mindfulness practices.* Meditation and other mindfulness practices that help you take charge of your thoughts can prove very useful as part of your anxiety-management program. The better you grasp the idea that the contents of your mind create suffering and the more fully you can release those thoughts, the less anxiety you will experience.

- *Guided imagery.* Guided imagery is a technique in which you guide yourself to calmness by mentally picturing a calming image or series of images. You might picture yourself on a blanket at the beach, walking by a lake, or swinging on a porch swing. First, determine what images actually calm you by trying out various images in your mind's eye. Then, when you've come up with some calming images, bring them to mind when you're feeling anxious.

- *Disidentification and detachment techniques.* A great way to reduce your anxiety is by learning to bring a calm, detached perspective to life and by turning yourself into someone whose default approach is to create calm rather than to create drama and stress. You do this in part by affirming that you are different from and larger than any transitory part of your life: any feeling, any thought, any worry, any regret, any family drama. By taking a more philosophical and detached approach, you can meet life more calmly.

- *Reorienting techniques.* You can consciously reorient yourself away from anxiety-producing stimuli and toward neutral or positive stimuli. For example, if your parents are fighting, you can put on your noise-canceling headphones and listen to music you love.

- *Discharge techniques.* When anxiety and stress build up in the body, techniques that vent that stress can prove very useful. One discharge technique is to silently scream — to make the facial gestures that go with uttering a good, cleansing scream without actually uttering a sound (which would be inappropriate in most settings). Jumping jacks, push-ups, and physical gestures of all sorts can be used to help pass the venom of anxiety out of your system.

- *Flipping the calmness switch.* Last but not least, try the following visualization. Picture yourself "flipping your calmness switch" and deciding to become a calmer person. Create a mental picture of that calmness switch: say something to yourself along the lines of "I

genuinely want to feel calmer," and imagine flipping
that switch in the direction of calmness.

～～～～～～～～～～～～～～～～～～～～～～～～

Consider that last technique. It's odd, but you can become
genuinely calmer just by deciding to become calmer. When
something happens to raise your anxiety level today, whether
it's a problem at work, something you encounter in the news,
one of your chronic pestering thoughts, or something agitating
that occurs in your family, take a deep breath and say, "No. I am
practicing calmness. I've flipped my calmness switch, and I can
deal with this calmly."

When that thing that your mate does that always drives
you crazy is about to drive you crazy for the millionth time and
provoke a fight that you know will lead nowhere, say, "No. I am
practicing calmness. I've flipped my calmness switch, and I can
deal with this calmly."

When you feel terrible heaviness and emptiness during a
family visit, when you know that the deep sadness that dogs
your heels is about to overwhelm you, rather than rushing off
manically to do something to forestall that feeling or taking to
your bed and pulling the covers over your head, say, "No. I am
practicing calmness. I've flipped my calmness switch, and I can
deal with this calmly."

Many people are trying to function in the middle of perpetual chaos, busyness, and inner turmoil. They run hard all
day, commuting, handling work responsibilities, picking up
their kids, shopping for meals, and simultaneously dealing
with everything else that life throws at them, from health issues
to bill payments to family crises to the state of their yard. Who

can stay centered or even catch their breath nowadays? Where is calmness in that picture?

This chaos and overwhelm only increase if you are also dealing with intense family difficulties. Conversely, this perpetual chaos makes an already difficult family situation worse. Maybe you might be able to focus on your child's school difficulties, your mate's coldness, or your aging parent's daily demands if you weren't also obliged to handle a hundred other tasks, chores, and challenges. You may be just barely able to get items checked off your perpetual to-do list and keep your life afloat — but you're doing it at the cost of your emotional and physical health and with the added, unfortunate result that your serious family difficulties go unattended.

CEREMONY: Locating Calm with a Snow Globe

Take some time each day, or a few times each day, for the following ceremony. Purchase a snow globe if you don't already have one. Shake it up. As the snow settles, breathe deeply, and say or think, "I am settling," "I am calming down," or some other phrase of your own choosing that helps you articulate that you now feel calmer. You can enact this ceremony with an actual snow globe — you can even have one fabricated to your specifications — or you can enact it as a mind ceremony, shaking up an imaginary snow globe and watching it settle in your mind's eye.

To achieve calmness in the face of multiple challenges, it is imperative that you identify a few anxiety-management techniques that work for you and practice them. You want to feel confident that you can calm your nerves before, say, having a hard discussion with your child or your mate. If you lack that confidence and you don't know how to handle your nerves, you're likely to avoid that conversation once again.

Make a concerted effort to bring calmness into your life by enacting the snow globe ceremony daily, by learning to flip your calmness switch, and by practicing anxiety-management techniques. Anxiety is a given; calmness is an acquired skill, one that you really need and one that you can work on and get better at.

Adding Calmness to Your Tool Kit

1. What in your current family situation agitates you and raises your anxiety level? What can possibly be done to change those dynamics?

2. Name some ways that you would like to grow calmer, and identify the steps you mean to take in order to get calmer.

CHAPTER FOUR

Being Clear

Family communication is often murky, negative, and hurtful. Much remains unsaid or half-said; and the things that are said are likely to be delivered with a critical edge. Surprisingly often, when someone in a family speaks, someone else in the family gets hurt. You can't change this dynamic single-handedly, but you can become an instrument for change.

Waiting for someone else in your family to begin communicating well won't work. If you wait for your child to reveal what's really on her mind, she's likely to continue keeping her fears, frustrations, and problems a secret. If you wait for your mate to start the communication ball rolling, you'll have another long wait coming. While it's true that every family member has a duty to communicate well, someone has to start. Let that person be you.

It's important that you say things directly, in short, simple, clear sentences. Saying things indirectly or at great length often means that you feel you don't have a leg to stand on, that you are ambivalent about your message, or that you hope the family member you're talking to won't discover your hidden agenda. It is better to be clear before you speak, know what you want to say, trust that you have the right to communicate, and then deliver your message simply and directly.

Here are some examples of clear, direct speaking:

- "You've been spending a lot of extra time at work. Does that mean that we have a problem?"
- "You seem to have much less homework this year than last year. Is that the case? Or are you less motivated this year?"
- "I want to stop working and start a home business. I know that has a lot of ramifications, but I'd like us to talk about it."
- "We've been having sex pretty infrequently. I wonder what's up."
- "You and your sister have been fighting a lot recently. Can you tell me what's going on?"
- "I feel like we need a vacation, but I know we don't have money put aside for that. Can we talk about whether we have any vacation options?"

Being direct isn't the same as being blunt or mean. Always leave room for kindness in the spaces between words. By your tone, your inflection, your body language, and by the words themselves, you can communicate the fact that you have something to say but that you don't mean to hurt, insult, or criticize the other person. If you pay attention to being both direct and kind, you will grow stronger as a communicator and also invite more love into every family interaction.

CEREMONY: Gaining Clarity

When you feel a lack of clarity about some situation in your family life, write on a sheet of paper, "There's something going on that I don't understand." Close your eyes and breathe regularly for a minute or two. Don't strain to gain clarity or to understand. Just relax. Then open your eyes and write below your first sentence, "I think what's going on is ___," and see how you want to complete that sentence. If nothing comes, or if what comes doesn't seem to be quite right or on point, repeat the ceremony. Close your eyes again, and breathe regularly. Open them after a few minutes and write out that sentence again: "I think what's going on is ___," and see how you want to complete it. If nothing comes, try this ceremonial exercise another time or two. If you gain some clarity, excellent! If not, congratulate yourself for showing up, and pledge to continue your efforts at gaining clarity.

Avoid Mixed Messages

Human beings send mixed messages all the time, especially within the family. A mixed message is a message in which two contradictory ideas are blithely — and often bizarrely — conjoined. Here are some classic mixed messages:

- "Please get all of your homework done and get to bed early."
- "I really want to have sex with you tonight, but I'm just not in the mood."

- "Grandpa, I'd love to visit you over spring break, but I only have a week off."
- "My job is killing me. By the way, I've asked to take on a couple of new assignments."
- "Mom, I really think we should eat healthier meals, but can we have cheeseburgers and fries tonight?"

Sometimes we can tell what is illogical or contradictory about a mixed message, and sometimes we can't quite. But we always know that they feel wrong. The reason we send mixed messages is that the truth is inconvenient or unpleasant. We find receiving mixed messages unacceptable for exactly the same reason: the sender has played fast and loose with the truth. Don't send mixed messages: be brave and tell the truth. Don't accept mixed messages, either: be smart and demand the truth.

It's your job to send clear messages. But what if the message sent to you isn't clear? Then your job is to ask for clarification. When you don't understand the message you just received, always ask. But be careful, because our first impulse is to criticize the sender for not being clear, or to lash out because we didn't like the message received.

Our most common response — "What did you mean by that?" — is often just an attack question and not a request for clarification at all. Its translation is, "How dare you say that!" All of the following are better alternative ways of asking for clarification.

- "I think you're saying ___, but I'm not positive. Am I close?"
- "There was a part there that I don't think I understood. What did you mean when you said ___?"
- "I'm a little confused. I think you said ___. But you also said ___. Did I get that right?"

- "I think I understand what you're saying, but I'm not 100 percent sure. Could you tell me a little more?"

Asking for clarification is an excellent communication skill that prevents small and large misunderstandings. If your daughter says, "My biology teacher is stupid," don't leap to the conclusion that your daughter is failing biology. Ask for clarification instead. She may only mean that in her opinion her biology teacher is stupid for giving homework on the weekend and so many pop quizzes, but she plans to get an A in biology as her revenge. Wasn't that good to clear up?

Be clear, don't send or accept mixed messages, and ask for clarification when you don't understand. Also, trust your intuition. When you have an intuition that a problem exists — that your son is in trouble, your husband is angry with you, or your sister is in crisis — you shouldn't ignore that feeling. Almost always, that intuition is right on the money. Trust your intuition that something is up, decide what you want to say, prepare yourself to say it, and then courageously hold that conversation.

Becoming a communication wizard may not enable you to cure everything that ails your family, but it may help a lot. Often, dramatic changes occur when what needs to be said gets said. Be clear about your intention to speak compassionately and forthrightly, be clear when you speak, and say exactly what you want to say and what you need to say. That clarity may work wonders!

Six Tips for Being Clear

- *Be clear about what you need.* Do you need your privacy? Do you need to be treated with respect? Do you

need to not have your efforts belittled? Do you need
to feel safe? Do you need some occasional praise? Do
you need help? Be clear both about what you need and
about how you will announce those needs!

• *Be clear about what you want.* Are you hoping for a
certain island vacation? Would you love a little more
tenderness, a little more romance, and a little more
kindness? Do you want to be able to watch your favorite television program without anyone making snide
remarks about it? Be clear about what you want and
about how you will announce those wants!

• *Be clear about what you won't tolerate.* Be clear about
what absolutely crosses the line. Maybe you've decided
to live with your mate's sardonic style, which always
verges on sarcasm — but how sarcastic is he or she
permitted to be? Be clear about what you won't tolerate and about how you will announce what you won't
tolerate!

• *Be clear about pointing out when a commitment or a
promise has been broken.* Is your mate chronically late?
Did you parents promise to help financially and then
conveniently forget — again? Did your teenager pledge
to never smoke cigarettes again — and come home
with clothes smelling of tobacco smoke? Be clear that
a promise has been broken and about what you intend
to say and do about it!

• *Be clear about who is supposed to do what.* If your siblings are being super vague about who is supposed to
take your ailing parent to medical appointments, re-
sulting in your taking up the slack and the bulk of the
responsibility, announce that their vagueness is not

okay with you. If your mate refuses to hire someone to do something that he says he can do, and then he doesn't do it, be clear about what you want to say and do. For instance, give him one more chance, and then hire someone!

- *Be clear about what matters.* Perhaps it doesn't matter if your mate is five minutes late and has a good reason, and perhaps it really does matter if he or she is an hour late and offers up the lamest of excuses. Distinguish between the two situations. In the first case, quickly let go of your irritation. In the second case, say what you need to say and do what you need to do. Be clear about what matters and about what you will say and do when something important has transpired!

~~~~~~

Adding Clarity to Your Tool Kit

1. What in your current family situation feels murky and unclear? What might you try in order to gain clarity on that issue, dynamic, or situation?
2. Name some ways that you would like to gain clarity. Next, identify the steps you mean to take in order to do so.

CHAPTER FIVE

Being Aware

Family difficulties tend to escalate if no one is paying attention to them, and this makes them harder to address later. It is relatively easy to remove an unwanted sapling from your garden. It is much harder and more expensive to remove an unwanted full-grown tree. In order to remove the sapling while it is still of manageable size, someone has to notice its existence and realize that it will grow into a tree that may threaten the house's foundation.

~~~~~~

Four Tips for Paying Close Attention

Awareness has both a noticing component and a predicting component. Being aware means both spotting something and also predicting its importance. Here are four tips for paying close attention:

1. *Ask whether core values are in question, or only little things.* If you're looking for things to be upset about,

you can always find them. You could spend your whole life upset with your husband's unwillingness to clean out the garage, your wife's anxiety attacks when company is coming, your sister's way of "borrowing" your clothes, or the face your dad makes when you don't get your chores done. Try to pay attention to whether a small thing is at stake or whether a big thing is at stake; paying attention in that way puts you in a position to make smarter decisions about when and how much to react to a situation.

It really doesn't pay to sweat the small things. On the other hand, it is vital that you speak and act when your core values are involved. Do you know what your core values are? One might be that you refuse to be abused in any way. If and when that happens, you will speak up immediately or take some appropriate action.

Sometimes we think that our core values are involved because of the way we construct our inner language. When a chore doesn't get done by a family member, we may feel not only upset but even betrayed. But while neglected chores constitute a problem, speaking to yourself in terms of betrayal and anger is a bigger problem. It leads to a sense of outrage and other catastrophic feelings when only a misdemeanor has occurred. Make sure that your core values really have been violated before you jump to high drama.

2. *Pay close attention to whether everyone in the family is getting a chance to speak and be heard.* It isn't solely your responsibility to be alert to family dynamics of this sort, but if no one else is watching out for them, you may have to take the lead. Maybe your youngest

child feels that what she has to say is never taken seriously, or maybe Dad feels he isn't as articulate as other family members. These simmering resentments are bound to boil over and might be nipped in the bud if you take some action now.

Say that the issue is where to go on your family vacation. To make sure that everyone gets a voice in the discussion, try the following. Have everyone write down their ideas, and then give the family copies of all of the sheets of paper and time to think about them. Next, call a family meeting and make sure that everyone's ideas are treated respectfully.

If someone isn't speaking, ask that person for their thoughts and feelings. It may be that the final decision necessarily rests with Mom and Dad, but it's still empowering for everyone to feel they've had their say. Occasionally ask yourself, "Does it feel like everybody in this household is being heard?" If someone's voice is being silenced or someone else's voice is dominating, pay attention to that and do something about it.

3. *Notice when and if stress is doing the talking.* One of the biggest problems that families face is trying to communicate lovingly and effectively when everyone is stressed out. Adults may be stressed by the demands of their jobs, by their commutes, and by money worries; the kids may be stressed by school and because the adults are stressed. In these circumstances, is it any wonder that family communication often consists mostly of angry outbursts?

Be alert to the ways that stress may be doing the

talking in your family and try the following to create
more patient interchanges:

- Get centered before you speak, especially before
  you're about to say something that you suspect will
  come out sounding abrasive or critical.
- Think before you speak: What are you really trying
  to say, and how do you want to say it?
- Try to speak from a place of love, not irritation.
- Be empathic and try to care about your listener,
  even if you're feeling stressed.
- Admit to being stressed — let family members
  know your reality.
- Try to reduce the stress in your life. Learn a few
  stress-management techniques and be alert to the
  amount of stress in your household.

4. *Notice whether family members' fears are being acknowledged.* People fear all sorts of things: public speaking,
   flying, driving at night, or even just going out alone.
   They fear upcoming exams, performance evaluations
   at work, getting fired, or even a visit from the in-laws.
   You and the other members of your family all have
   fears, and those fears may be causing or exacerbating
   your current difficulties.

   If you're paying close attention and become aware
   that someone in your family is afraid of something,
   what should you do? It rarely helps to say, "Don't
   worry," or "There's nothing to fear." It's better to ask
   if there's anything you can do to help, wonder aloud if
   talking about it might be of some use, share your own

fears, or describe a technique you use to manage your own anxiety. All of these are better than telling your loved one that he or she is "wrong" to be afraid.

Many difficult family situations occur because someone in the family is afraid of something and doesn't want to reveal that fear to anyone else. Your daughter, for all her bravado, may be afraid of getting behind the wheel for the first time. Your son may be afraid that his grades, while still excellent, have slipped just far enough that he's ruined his chances of getting into his first-choice college. Your husband may be afraid that his failure to adequately prepare for retirement means he'll have to keep working forever. These fears affect family life tremendously, and they are among the hardest things for people to talk about, even those who love one another.

You can help in all these regards by being aware. Yes, paying this much attention sets the bar very high. But it is also a family blessing for someone to pay this much good attention — a blessing that will serve your family and, in turn, serve you.

~~~~~~

My client Anna told me she thought that her daughter Rebecca loved to sing in her church choir and her school musicals. In retrospect, Anna realized that perhaps she kept pressing her daughter to perform because she loved Rebecca's singing. She didn't realize how tense Rebecca got before performances, especially important ones like the annual school pageant — to the point of being physically ill.

Before one major performance, Rebecca broke down. She started sharing her suicidal thoughts and revealed that she'd begun cutting herself. These revelations led to a psychiatric evaluation, which led to a clinical diagnosis, which led to psychiatric medication — and when the first medication had adverse side effects, it led to other psychiatric medications. Rebecca was eventually hospitalized several times. To say that this downhill slide occurred because Anna was unaware of how profoundly singing stressed out her daughter is of course to oversimplify the situation. But who's to say that better awareness there might not have helped reduce the pressure Rebecca was experiencing?

CEREMONY: Increasing Awareness

Try the following ceremony to help increase your awareness. First, make the decision to stop everything for half an hour. Put your electronics away and find a quiet place. Take a few deep breaths and say silently or out loud, "I am willing to see what is actually going on." Announce your willingness to know the truth, even if the truth is difficult.

Then pick a family member, say your sister Jane, and say, "What should I be aware of with regard to Jane?" Give yourself a chance to really be with the question. Open up to Jane's truth and reality. Write down what you learn. Continue this process with other family members, including you.

Then turn to family situations. You might ask yourself, "What should I be aware of with regard to our finances?" or "What should I be aware of with regard to family communication?" Patiently sit with each such question, bravely investigate the reality of each situation, and write down what you learn.

Then read what you've written and ask yourself, "What actions flow from what I just learned?" Write down your responses and try to decide which of those actions you are ready and willing to take.

When you're done with this ceremony, congratulate yourself for having bravely gained better awareness about what's really going on in your life and in the lives of other family members. Calmly leave your quiet space and, if you feel equal to it, take one of the actions on your action list. Even if you don't feel equal to acting, congratulate yourself on having faced life with some real attention and awareness!

The keys to awareness are patience and willingness. We are typically impatient, defensive participants in our lives, embroiled in our situations rather than detached enough from them to see what's really going on. This happens in part because we are busy, and also because we are defensive and do not want to acknowledge the part we ourselves are playing in our family dramas. Impatient and defensive, we avoid noticing that our spouse refuses to honor agreements, that our sister is rail-thin, or that we are having more and more trouble getting out of bed each morning. As a result, nothing changes and nothing improves. Improving family life requires your awareness.

Adding Awareness to Your Tool Kit

1. What aspect of your current family situation deserves or requires your full attention and awareness? What might you try to do in order to bring your awareness to that issue, dynamic, or situation?

2. Name some ways that you would like to become more aware. Next, identify the steps you mean to take in order to do so.

CHAPTER SIX

Being Brave

Often we feel too weak to deal with a family difficulty, like a bullying sibling, or with the results of having grown up in our particular family, like chronic sadness. At such times we need to manifest our strength if we are to thrive or even just survive.

At other times we feel afraid, and that fear prevents us from effectively taking care of ourselves or improving our situation. Then we need to manifest our courage. Many people feel afraid inside because they are physically or verbally abused. Or they may feel as though they have to walk on eggshells so as not to provoke criticism or an outburst. They move through their house — and their lives — silently and stealthily.

Sometimes the fear may sound rather odd. I had a client who was afraid to come home from work. He wasn't physically afraid of his wife — it was nothing like that. What he feared was realizing all over again that he didn't love her or even like her, that they weren't suited to be together, and that sooner or later, and despite the fact that they had two small children, they would have to divorce.

It may seem odd to describe this reaction as fear, but that's exactly what it felt like to my client. The prospect of going home after work each day — or rather, the prospect of what he would realize the instant he stepped inside the door — terrified him.

When we began working together, he didn't understand that he had this issue. He described his problems in other ways, saying, for instance that he was a workaholic who put in the most hours of any lawyer at his law firm; that he was obsessed with fitness and as a result spent too many hours at the gym, thus neglecting his home life; that, like so many lawyers, he had great difficulty balancing work and family; and that he had trouble making and keeping friends, a problem he had made an effort to solve by setting up frequent after-work social events at various local watering holes.

Nowhere in the presentation of his perceived difficulties was there a hint of any fear of going home — or any fear at all. Yet after just a session or two, it became clear to both of us that not only did he hate going home, but going home actually frightened him. He could feel the anxiety and fear well up in him as the day progressed and quitting time approached. To deal with that fear, he would stay as late as possible at the office, go to a bar and socialize, or go directly to the gym.

This new knowledge shed a bright light on his behaviors. Once he understood what was going on, he had to face the fact that he hated his marriage and that it terrified him to own up to that truth.

Over a couple of months, we worked on his showing courage in two specific ways. First, he had to bravely go home at an appropriate time every day, if only because his children needed him. Second, he had to bravely bring up with his wife — and also more fully with himself — the fact that their marriage wasn't working.

Neither proved easy. He found reasons to stay late at work, such as "My annual review is approaching, and my bonus hinges on how many hours I put in." Likewise, he found it hard to muster the courage to contemplate ending his marriage. Although he continued to work long hours, he eventually renewed his commitment to his marriage, he and his wife entered counseling, and he began to relish spending time with his children.

~~~~~~

Tip: Accessing Your Truth

You may have a similar sort of trouble even knowing that something in your family life is frightening you. You may have framed your reluctance to come home from school as a dread of the walk home rather than as the fear of coming home to an empty house. You may have named your inability to get work done at home as attention deficit disorder rather than as your fear of asking family members to be quiet. How can you come to know that you are frightened of something if you don't currently have access to that knowledge? One way to find out is to patiently ask yourself and endeavor to answer the following question: "Might there be something that I'm afraid of that I don't know that I'm afraid of?"

~~~~~~

You want to be brave inside your family, but you also want to be safe. This is an enduring dilemma in human life: whether to stand up to a danger or to opt for discretion over valor. If, for example, you're in a physically abusive relationship, leaving is likely far wiser than being "brave" in a confrontational way. Or rather, leaving may in fact be the act of courage: it may require all your courage to accept the consequences of leaving, which might include losing your financial security and completely uprooting your life.

The bravery that we need to manifest with respect to our family life may not necessarily be physical. Instead it may take the form of saying something that it scares us to say, making a hard decision, or looking courageously at something that frightens us.

Marcia, a client, used my focused-journal method to help herself grow braver. One step of that process is examining whether or not you've reached the heart of the issue you're exploring. Here is a portion of her journal:

Entry 1

I know I want to be brave. But have I gotten to the heart of the matter by the way I've framed the issue? Yes and no. I do want to be brave with my family. I have a lot of things that I want to say to my siblings. But I don't want them to get mad at me. That's a very deep fear.

I devoted so much time to caring for and worrying about our mother while my siblings went about living their lives. Since her death, they only call when they need something from me. Even my brother — who moved in with us after Mom died — can't seem to talk to me unless he wants something (are you going to make dinner?). So

I do want to be brave. I want to speak up and tell them that I want them to care about me and not what I can do for them.

I am not a substitute for Mom just because I am 13, 16, and 19 years older than them. I need some personal bravery to speak my mind and risk losing the only family I have (other than my husband). I need to just speak up because this feeling of being taken advantage of and not being cared for is making me upset.

I haven't really had a relationship with the three of them anyway, so why does it worry me so much? My relationship with my husband means more to me than being friends with my siblings. But I'm scared — why? The worst that will happen is that I will be alone with my husband, and that was where I was before Mom died. Huh, seems so simple now.

Entry 2

On January 1, I gave my brother a deadline date to move out. One of our sisters offered him a room, and I suggested that he take it. He got mad and moved out immediately. And to my surprise — the sky did not fall down on me! In fact, a large weight feels like it lifted from my shoulders.

After thinking about this and realizing that the sky had not fallen from my brother moving on, I managed to speak my mind to my family. My brother was already mad, so that didn't bother me. My sister is irate with me and blamed me for the lack of relationship. During that conversation I realized that we are just in two very different places. She may never understand, but that's okay.

We'll both live. My other sister and I had a lovely discussion, and she said some very nice things to me. Her view of our relationship was different (better) than mine had been. Since our talk, we have talked almost daily on the phone. I feel lighter now!

CEREMONY: Crossing the Deep Divide

If you learn that there is indeed something scaring you in your family life, how might you become braver? Try the following ceremony. Get two small scatter rugs and place them a few inches apart. Stand at the edge of one rug and face the second rug. Imagine that you are standing at the edge of a cliff with a deep gorge between you and the second rug. Feel the depth of that gorge and how terrifying it would be to fall that far down. But, as deep and as frightening as that gorge is, it only takes a small step to cross it. Take that small step from one rug to the other while thinking, "Many fears are like this."

Feel the deep comfort of arriving safely on the other side. A given fear — such as a fear that your marriage is untenable — may run deep, and may have run deep inside you for years and years. This ceremony can help remind you that you can step right over your fear by using a ceremonial bridge of this sort. Enact this ceremony, and then move on to the hard work that may follow.

How would you like to grow braver? Will you try some wild activity like skydiving or deep-sea diving? Will you stand in front of a mirror and practice and rehearse what you want and need to say to someone in your family? Will you take an assertiveness class, a self-defense class, or a martial arts class?

Will you create a visualization in which you see yourself as a brave warrior or as a brave person, an everyday samurai? Will you begin to say "Yes!" and "No!" in no uncertain terms? Will you, maybe by journaling, identify the injuries you have suffered and, with respect to each of those injuries, breathe and say, "That is behind me now"? Spend a little time thinking about how exactly you will grow braver.

Risks feel risky. Dangers feel dangerous. It is very easy to say "Be braver," but the risks and dangers of real life have a way of making us genuinely scared and inhibiting our ability to manifest our courage. You have that courage, but it may be hard to show it. Try. You might start by being brave in a not-too-dangerous situation. Take a small risk. However that turns out — even if you get scared — try again. Keep trying. Stand up for yourself — everywhere in life, but particularly inside your own family.

Adding Bravery to Your Tool Kit

1. Identify what in your current family situation feels dangerous and scary. What might you try in order to create more safety for yourself?
2. Name some ways that you would like to grow braver. Next, identify the steps you mean to take to do so.

CHAPTER SEVEN

Being Present

To deal effectively with a difficult family situation, you need to "be here now": you need to be present so that you can muster your strength, your courage, your clarity, and your smarts. If you're only half here, you're unlikely to find the motivation, the serenity, or the inner resources to cope.

Being present is hard. Most people are elsewhere: pestered by the past, lost in fantasy, or defensively distracted by the busy work and the busy thoughts that they create.

If you have two hours at your disposal and it is important to you that you have a certain difficult conversation with your teenage son, then it is not reasonable to plan on doing other things during that time, like weeding your garden, planning your menus for the week, catching up on the world news, or making sure that the storm windows are in good working order. In this context, all of those arguably reasonable activities are ways to avoid being present for that conversation with your son.

Nor is it useful during that time period to be *thinking* about weeding your garden, planning your menus for the week, catching up on the world news, or examining your storm windows — not if what you ought to be thinking about is what to say to your son. In these circumstances, those thoughts are deflections and distractions. They only help you avoid the hard work of dealing with your son.

If, on the other hand, you can be present, you can rehearse what you want to say to your son and rehearse your responses to his denials and justifications. You can do some internet research on your son's situation; you can practice an anxiety-management technique in anticipation of the stress the conversation may cause you; or you can quiet yourself, center yourself, and march right off to find your son and talk to him. Most of the time, it's fine to weed the garden or to think about weeding the garden — but not when you ought to be dealing with your son's problem.

In addition to our defensiveness and our desire to distract ourselves from the important business at hand, thoughts of the past can also impair our ability to be present. We know that it would serve us to think clearly about what might best help our son and what precisely we want to say to him; but when we try to do exactly that, instead of being able to focus on those important tasks, we find ourselves flooded with anguish about the past, filled with regrets about how we have let our son down over the years, or saddened by our past wrong turns and mistakes. Those unwanted, intrusive thoughts prevent us from really being here now. Suddenly we are remembering — and stewing about — something we did or failed to do twenty years ago, and we are left with no mind space to deal with our son's current pressing situation.

Dealing with our defensive distractibility and facing the unceremonious return of the past are lifelong challenges. We can make an effort to face them by holding the intention to be here now; by maintaining awareness of our very human penchant to fool ourselves, trick ourselves, and distract ourselves; by practicing calmness and thus reducing the anxiety that causes us to want to distract ourselves and flee; by engaging in a regular practice (like a meditation practice) whose objective is to teach us how to be here now; and by enacting ceremonies that help keep us present. We may never get perfect at being present, but we can make many improvements.

Tip: Coming Back to What's Important

To address your defensive distractibility, you might try the following. Think about a difficult challenge — in the example I've been using, that conversation you need to have with your son. As you try to engage with that challenge, notice where your thoughts want to go. Do they go to the past and your regrets? Do they go to some task that suddenly seems very urgent, like weeding your garden? Wherever they go, calmly but firmly say, "I need to come back to what's really important." If that phrase doesn't work for you, then pick another. Practice this exercise and see if you can gain some mastery over your wandering thoughts.

CEREMONY: Releasing Regrets

What if the past keeps returning? Say, for example, that certain regrets keep coming back to haunt you. Maybe you frequently find yourself regretting the wrong paths you took, the time you wasted, the opportunities you missed, the ways in which you failed yourself or failed others. The following is a powerful ceremony that I often present at my writing workshops to help writers heal their regrets. You might give it a try.

In addition to the regrets that we all harbor, writers harbor many additional ones: for example, regret that they haven't produced writing of a consistently high quality, that they haven't written as often or as much as they should have, or that they haven't had the publishing successes they dreamed of. I ask them to choose one of those poignant regrets, write it down on a sheet of paper, fold up the paper, tear the paper to shreds, and toss the shreds in the air while saying or thinking, "I am through with that regret!" This is a very powerful, useful ceremony that you can repeat as needed.

It is hard to be present, and doubly so in the face of difficulty. We are designed as much to flee as to stay put. And by being present I mean something that sets the bar very high: being present to that which really requires your attention. Focusing single-mindedly on what we happen to be doing — such as focusing on a potato as we peel it — is not being present in the sense we are discussing. Rather, we need to be present to what is important. If what you really need to do right now is have that conversation with your son, you need to be present to that reality and not to the potato.

Janice, a client, expressed concern about her teenage son's drinking. She wanted to confront him about it but didn't feel equal to that conversation. To help her experience how the conversation might go, I asked her to be present to it by rehearsing it in her mind's eye. People are often extremely accurate in these visualized rehearsals. When and if they manage to actually have the interaction, it usually goes exactly as they imagined it would go. I asked her to give it a try, and she agreed.

"What's first?" I asked.

"I have to make him sit down. He's always either coming and going or locked away in his room. I have to make him sit down on the living room sofa."

"Okay. He's passing by. What do you want to say to him?"

"Please sit down."

"Okay. He sits down, yes? Now what?"

She took a deep breath. "James, I think you have a problem with alcohol."

"What happens next?"

"He protests. He squirms. He denies everything."

"But he doesn't get up and leave?"

"No."

"Okay. Stay present. What's next?"

"I present my case. I tell him that I found his bottle of vodka in the freezer. That I smell alcohol coming off of him — that I smell alcohol coming through his pores. That he's secretive, not like a teenager, but like...an alcoholic. That he has hangovers." She stopped. "That's enough, I think."

"And how does he react?"

"He's quiet." She paused. "That's really hard, that he's quiet.

I want to keep speaking! I want to start yelling. That silence feels harder than anything he might say. I see…that I hate silence. I need to fill it up."

"And so?"

"And so I say nothing. I'm quiet too."

"What happens next?"

"I don't know. I can't see it."

"Okay. What do you need to say next?"

She thought about that. "Consequences," she said. "I need to tell him super clearly what I need him to do."

"And what is that?"

"Accompany me to an AA meeting." She glanced at me. "I could demand that he do other things, but I wouldn't know if he was doing them or not. But going to an AA meeting with me — that I would see with my own two eyes."

"And if he refuses?"

"I don't know." She got very quiet. "I don't want to present him with an ultimatum. I don't want him to leave home."

"Okay." I waited. "Then what?"

"If he refuses, I'll make it my business to have the conversation the next day, too. I'll be present to this real thing again the next day. And as many consecutive days as it takes."

"Okay. Thank you!"

Not every story like this has a happy ending, but this one did. When Janice sat James down, he admitted to his alcohol abuse, announced that he actually wanted to stop, accompanied his mother to several AA meetings, and then began to go to meetings on his own. This outcome could not have been achieved unless Janice had added being present to her family survival tool kit.

CEREMONY: Achieving Presence

Find a quiet place. Get comfortably seated and close your eyes. Ask yourself: "Where in my family life do I need to be more present?" Wait quietly as your mind considers the question. Even if nothing comes up, congratulate yourself for having made the effort. If something does come up, sit with it. Say, for example, that it's an issue between you and your mate. Engage in the kind of mental rehearsal that Janice did. In your mind's eye, be present to that interaction and see how it plays out. Then decide if you want to bravely risk that interaction for real. Whatever you decide, celebrate having done this important work!

Adding Presence to Your Tool Kit

1. Identify where in your family life you particularly lack presence. What might you try to do in order to become more present there?
2. Name some ways that you would like to be more present. Carefully identify the steps you mean to take to do so.

CHAPTER EIGHT

Being Resilient

Few human beings manage to completely avoid feelings of anger, sadness, hopelessness, pointlessness, or overwhelm. Many people experience these feelings a lot, especially when their family life is difficult. At any given moment in a troubled family, one family member may have lost hope for real change, a second may be experiencing deep fatigue, and a third may be engaged in self-destructive behavior, acting out the family's difficulties by getting drunk, for example, or driving recklessly.

If you are burdened by feelings of this sort or find yourself acting in ways that harm you, you need to manifest those qualities that we've been discussing, and another quality too: resilience. You need to be able to bounce back from all that! In a difficult family situation, feelings like sadness, anxiety, and hopelessness are givens. What is open to question is whether you can weather them and recover your balance.

Resilience is the willingness and the ability to bounce back. The *willingness* is as essential as the ability. It is common for a person to make the decision, somewhere just out of conscious awareness, that he doesn't want to bounce back — that because, in his estimation, he's been treated unfairly by life, he will stubbornly stay in some dark, angry, injured place. Rather than deciding to bounce back with renewed energy and renewed hope, and reconciling himself to some less-than-ideal set of changed circumstances, he pulls up the drawbridge and adopts a siege mentality. Being adamant in defeat amounts to self-harm: it is no sign of strength. And being resilient, even if that resilience sometimes involves humbling surrender, is no sign of weakness.

The following story illustrates an obstinacy that is the opposite of resilience. A client of mine, a writer who felt that his editor had rudely criticized the manuscript he turned in to her, refused to make the changes she demanded, changes that he himself felt might improve the book, on the principle that she had been too high-handed in delivering her criticisms. At first glance this may not seem like a family issue, but for a writer whose family is counting on his income and who has family responsibilities, it is.

By refusing to make even a single change, my client cost himself and his family a large amount of the advance money he was due to receive. He dug in his heels; the editor canceled the book contract; and soon thereafter my client had to hit the pavement looking for a day job to make up for that lost income. People dig in their heels — and dig themselves holes — just like this with quite amazing regularity, and in the process they make family life that much more difficult.

Resilience is the ability — and the willingness — to shake off slights, insults, criticism, and regrets for the sake of moving forward and living the best life possible.

CEREMONIES: Bringing Back Hope

If you are in fact willing to practice resilience — to bounce back and to not dig in your heels and stay in a dark place — this is a simple ceremony to try. Take any feeling that is burdening you — say, the feeling of hopelessness — and enact a ceremony to bring back hope. The very act of engaging in such a ceremony signals your willingness and desire to return to the game.

What sort of ceremony might you enact?

- You might make a batch of hope cookies and, as you prepare the batter, say or think, "I am still hopeful!"
- You might plant a hope garden and, as you water your garden, say or think, "I am still hopeful!"
- You might create a hope altar and, as you pay it your daily visit, say or think, "I am still hopeful!"

It is easy to lose hope — but we can recover it as part of our resilience program. Manifest your resilience by creating a different ceremony of healing for each of those tangled feelings — hopelessness, anger, boredom, worry — that weave together into your darkest moods.

You might also try the following. Identify music that suggests resilience and victory to you (perhaps the theme from the movie *Rocky*). Make it your theme song. Listen to it when you wake up, to start your day positively and powerfully. Listen to it at midday, to give yourself a boost before that afternoon slump hits. Listen to it at bedtime, to put yourself in the right frame of mind for a good night's sleep. Listen to it before a difficult interaction, whenever you feel defeated, or as a way to motivate yourself to make some necessary change. Use it as often as you need it!

Suppose you want to move to a less expensive part of the country so that you can quit your day job and live more simply and happily. However your husband, who has many objections to moving, refuses to have a real conversation with you about the subject. When you try to bring it up, he makes a face and leaves the room. Frustrated, angry, and resentful, you find that you are avoiding him, just as he is avoiding you.

It takes real resilience to try to have that conversation if you are rebuffed each time. It takes real resilience not to throw in the towel or throw up your hands but instead to think about how to move your agenda forward. For example, might he be willing to spend a weekend in the locale you have in mind? Might he be willing to listen to your arguments for moving if he heard them from your adult son or daughter? Might it help to point out all the golf courses or fishing streams he might get to enjoy if you moved?

All of these are reasonable tactics, but we tend not to try them because we internally say, "The heck with him and his attitude!" The better bet is to keep bouncing back, like a fighter who keeps getting off the ropes, so that you retain the chance to realize your dreams. Engage in your ceremony of hope, play your resilience theme song, and return to the fray!

We all receive blows from which we must bounce back and recover. In school we sometimes fail tests; in the job market we sometimes do not get hired; in relationships our love is sometimes not reciprocated. And even though we often manage to bounce back from setbacks and disappointments, we also change and decline emotionally as a result of these repeated blows.

Say, for example, that you make a loving gesture toward your mate, and the gesture isn't acknowledged, appreciated, or reciprocated. Probably you are resilient enough to try again. But if your gestures are rejected repeatedly, you start to grow sour and despairing. Very likely you begin to call yourself stupid for continuing to try, and you grow angry and resentful. Over time, you may lose your confidence, your optimism, and even your sense of life's meaning.

So the ideal of resilience is not only to be able to bounce back from the many blows inflicted upon us but also to be able to identify the bruises that those blows have caused, bruises that show up in such forms as negative self-talk, despair, and hopelessness. Even a basically self-assured, indefatigable person can be worn down by a lack of opportunity, a lack of success, interpersonal rejection, and other repeated blows to her self-esteem and her ability to make meaning.

Tips for Increasing Resilience

You can help yourself increase your resilience by trying any of the following:

- Think through what has helped you in the past to bounce back, such as the support of a certain friend, group support, journaling about the blow, giving yourself a pep talk, or engaging in a healing ritual.
- Think through things you haven't tried that might help. Is there a class or workshop on resilience that

seems attractive to you, a program of study, or a spiritual, mindfulness, or meditation practice?

- Recall a time when you recovered from a blow quickly and relatively painlessly. Why do you think bouncing back was easier that time? Were you so busy that you hardly noticed the blow? Was your self-talk more positive then than it is today? Were you in an intimate relationship that helped buffer the blow? Is there anything to learn from that experience?

What do you think helps people bounce back? List as many possibilities as you can dream up, and then take a stab at ranking them in importance. What rose to the top of your list? Would you care to give it a try when you need to pull resilience out of your tool kit?

~~~~~~

Adding Resilience to Your Tool Kit

1. What in your current family situation requires that you manifest resilience?
2. Name some ways that you would like to grow more resilient. Next, identify the steps you mean to take in order to achieve that new resilience.

PART TWO

Ten Difficult Family Types

n part 2 of this book I introduce ten types of families that are difficult in their own particular ways. Of course, no real family exactly matches any of these types: no family is exclusively sad and anxious, at war, bullying, or loveless, for example. But families do have their enduring challenges and characteristic colorations. Looking at difficult family types is useful in understanding why family life is so perilous and taxing.

We can't help but internalize and be affected by what's going on around us, whether that all happened long ago in childhood or is happening right now in our current family. If your daily life revolves around a family member's addiction, if your predominant feeling is one of not being loved, if your actions are circumscribed by rigid rules and your every move is scrutinized, you need to make real use of your tool kit or else risk long-term emotional harm. Identifying the types of problems that occur in your family is an important step toward dealing with them.

CHAPTER NINE

Sad and Anxious Families

Sadness, unhappiness, and despair (typically called depression nowadays) and feelings of anxiety and worry (which, like sadness, nowadays typically result in a diagnosis of a mental disorder and a pharmaceutical intervention) are epidemic worldwide — and have always been epidemic.

It is human to despair, and it is human to worry. But when either of these realities, or both at once, becomes the predominant coloration of family life, then you must contend both with your sad and anxious family members and with your own "sympathetic" sadness and anxiety.

Typically, sad families make us sad, and anxious families make us anxious. Of course, life isn't quite that simple: sometimes we react to the anxiety and edginess of somebody in our family by refusing to worry, by taking risks, and in other ways trying to fight off the family anxiety. Or we may try to deal with the sadness in our family by putting on a false smile and acting as if everything were perfectly fine — by becoming a

Pollyanna — and developing stomachaches, headaches, and other forms of mental and physical distress as we try to fool ourselves into a happiness that we do not actually feel.

Because it is surprisingly difficult for a human to openly admit to being sad or anxious, these feelings in your family may never be made explicit, either by those who experience them or by other family members who must deal with the consequences of those hidden feelings. It is extremely rare, for example, for a parent to come home from work and say to the family, "I am feeling very sad today," or "I am feeling very anxious today." It is considerably more likely that the parent will start drinking, find something around the house to be upset about, demand that everyone be quiet so that he or she can watch television, shrink away for some private time, or act out his or her distress in some other way without frankly reporting it.

This unreported and unacknowledged anxiety and despair inevitably affects you. And there may be some sense, about which we currently know nothing and which may forever elude research, in which you yourself were born a little sadder or a little more anxious than the next person. If that's the case, it may also be true for other members of your family. That means you are confronted by two separate but related challenges: the sadness and anxiety that are part of your original personality, and the sadness and anxiety that you have acquired through family life that are part of your formed personality.

Chronic Family Sadness and Anxiety

Family therapists, who believe that individual problems must be viewed in a family context, tend to think of states like sadness and anxiety as either acute or chronic. Acute anxiety and sadness come and go and relate to actual events and particular circumstances. Chronic anxiety and sadness, by contrast, are pretty much always there: they affect family life on a daily basis.

Your father may be sad because he just lost his job, or he may be sad because sadness is the background coloration of his life. The first state is acute or situational, and the second is chronic and often intergenerational: the basic coloration of his family of origin may have been one of sadness, too.

Likewise, your sister may be anxious because she has to perform in her school play, or she may be anxious because she was born with or has acquired a generally anxious nature. The first expression of anxiety is situational and will pass once the performance is over; the second is persistent and maybe even pervasive, and it will affect everyone in the family.

If you grew up or are now living in a sad or anxious family (or both), it's likely that you too have become chronically sad and anxious. Do you experience these feelings in response to concrete and specific events, like an upcoming test or a job review, or are they a chronic coloration of your life, part of the contours of your original personality and your family experience?

Family therapists see families as incubators of chronic conditions like anxiety and sadness. The therapists Steven Harris and Dean Busby explain how Murray Bowen's family systems theory, which sees families as "closed systems" where every action and interaction affects everyone in the family, conceptualizes family anxiety.

Every individual and family experience two types of "anxiety" throughout the course of life: acute anxiety and chronic anxiety. Chronic anxiety is transmitted generationally. Acute anxiety, by contrast, occurs when significant psychosocial stressors happen in the life of an individual or family system. An example of acute anxiety is the birth or death of a family member, a child leaving home to go to college, a life-threatening event or some other experience that occurs within the system. Family systems theory assigns less importance to traumatic events in understanding an individual's emotional development than it does to ongoing family process. Events may highlight some aspects of the nature of the process, but the events are not the process.

What this means for you is that you may find yourself sad or anxious in the absence of particular events that cause such feelings. In your everyday life, you are likely to feel sad and anxious by virtue of the fact that the extended family system promotes those feelings. In turn, your feelings maintain the family's high levels of sadness and anxiety. This cycle is common in difficult families, yours included.

Being Yourself in a Sad or Anxious Family

What can you do if sadness and anxiety are circulating in your family system? You can manifest the eight skills we discussed in the first eight chapters:

- *Be smart.* Both sadness and anxiety are part of the human picture: these twin demons are not leaving our species anytime soon. It is smart to accept their reality and to resolve that you will deal with them openly and honestly.
- *Be strong.* Sadness and anxiety in your family weaken all family members, who likely find themselves tiptoeing

around, muffling their energy, and dimming their passion as a result. To counteract this tendency, practice your strength skills every day, just as if you were in training for a marathon or an Olympic event.

- *Be calm.* If you're dealing with a family made up of anxious people whose jitters and never-ending worries color your days, then you have the job of not falling into line with their anxious natures and of being diligent about practicing calmness in the midst of all that upsetting energy. If anxiety surrounds you, no skill is more important to practice than being calm.

- *Be clear.* Take the time to educate yourself about the current controversies in the mental health field. For example, it will make a huge difference in your life whether you conclude that you and other family members are experiencing a biological malfunction of some sort or whether your feelings are your natural reaction to life experiences.

- *Be aware.* Notice what's really going on around you. If your mother takes to her bed with some unnamed ailment, be aware that it may be despair and not illness sending her there. If your brother starts complaining about his teachers, be aware that he may be sad and despondent about a decline in his grades. If your grandmother begins to make excuses about why she can't visit often, look for the anxiety that creeps in as people age. Sadness and anxiety may be lurking or hiding in your family life much more often than you think!

- *Be brave.* If your mom or your brother is despairing, but that despair hasn't been named or acknowledged, you might want to bravely be the one to say to your mom, "You are so sad, you must try something," or to your brother, "Jack, I know how unhappy you are. Can we please talk about it?" It takes courage to say this, especially if the sadness is a family secret, but you can do it if you manifest your bravery.

- *Be present.* It is hard to be present in the midst of anxiety. Our first reaction to finding ourselves in an environment permeated by anxiety is to flee. If your family gives off anxious vibes, it will take you real effort to stay present, centered, and grounded when you're around them. When you notice that you want to flee your family, say to yourself, "I can stay here and be present, even though they are making me feel anxious!"

- *Be resilient.* If sadness and anxiety have infiltrated your system and are now a part of your formed personality, or if they are part of your original personality, then they will keep returning to challenge you, and you will need to use your resilience to deal with them. Remember: a truly resilient you can deal with the challenge of sadness and anxiety returning!

Marty and Maryanne

Marty and his wife, Maryanne, had both been diagnosed as depressed and were on antidepressants. Those chemicals had added all sorts of complications to an already desperate situation. Maryanne had gone from skinny to obese; Marty had regular and severe physical problems that he'd never had before, which required almost weekly medical appointments; and their already tenuous love life had dwindled to a complete zero.

Maryanne, a writer, came to see me in my capacity as a creativity coach. She'd been working on her memoir for several years without making much progress. Almost at the outset, I wondered aloud to what extent sadness and anxiety might be holding her back. The question surprised her, but only for a moment. She quickly agreed that sadness and anxiety, not only hers but also her husband's and, tragically, her grown sons', were impeding her progress. The darkness in the family, she suddenly saw, had cast a pall over everything and extinguished her desire to write.

In addition to the other tactics I proposed, including instituting a morning writing practice and regular email check-ins with me on her writing progress, I suggested that Maryanne familiarize herself with the eight skills and, if she felt able to take that next step, begin to practice those skills so as to reduce her own sadness and anxiety and maybe also exert some positive influence on her family. She agreed and began by translating each skill into "a change I want to make."

She translated "Be smart" into "I want to learn about antidepressants and about depression, gain my own personal understanding of whether or not I have a 'mental disorder' or whether I am just very sad. And if it looks like we're really talking about sadness, I want to see what I can do to figure out the sources of my sadness and figure out what I can do to reduce it."

She translated "Be present" into "I can't write if I'm too anxious to be present to the writing and if I'm continually running away from the writing. Therefore I'm going to learn one or two anxiety-management strategies and use them to quiet myself before a writing session, when I'm always so resistant and nervous and bothered by negative thoughts, and also during a writing session, when so much of the time all I want to do is get up and run away."

Patiently she translated all eight of the skills into "change sentences" and began the brave work of becoming more aware of her personality, her circumstances, and her ingrained habits, and of making small but real changes. She eventually came to the conclusion that she did not have a mental disorder but rather a lifelong gloomy outlook that was rooted in her parents' failures, their lack of love and approval of her, and her regrets about her largest decisions, including choosing a profession that paid the bills and allowed her to write but which she hated.

She realized that she could not change the past. But she could, with medical guidance, come off antidepressants; she could begin the long but necessary process of changing her profession; she could get a better grip on her thoughts, both generally and for the sake of her writing; and she could institute all sorts of new practices and habits, including regular writing and exercise regimens. These efforts, while they didn't make her flat-out happy, made her feel proud of herself and occasionally experience something like deep happiness for the first time she could remember.

Little of her effort rubbed off on her husband or on her sons. Their dramas, antics, anxiety attacks, and bouts of sadness continued. She wished she could do more for them and talk them into joining her in her new attitudes and practices, but she came to realize that not only were they not interested in her help or on board with her program, but they actually resented the changes and progress she was making.

Her husband complained that her new, careful eating was depriving him of his only fun, eating out with her. Her older son complained that now that she was back to writing her memoir, she was bound to divulge family secrets and ruin the family, and her younger son managed to get into two car accidents in a month, accidents that she believed were connected to her trying to improve herself.

Nevertheless, she remained resolute. She understood that she could not control her family and that even influencing them didn't seem to be in the cards. She had to take care of herself first. It was clear to her that she'd never really done that before, and that all of the gloom, negativity, and free-floating anxiety of her childhood had somehow subdued and weakened her. Now she intended to be strong. Although she hoped that what she was doing for herself might eventually help her family, first she had to manage her own journey.

CEREMONY: Creating Your Life-Purpose Icon

If you're sad because you've grown up or are living in a sad family, or for other reasons, one thing that can really help you feel less sad is identifying your life purposes and living them. Doing this will help with your anxiety as well. We feel less sad and less anxious when we are living as though we matter.

However, it can be hard to remember your life purposes as life rushes along and you get caught up in everyday issues of survival and daily chores and responsibilities. Try creating your own life-purpose icon to remind you of your life purposes and your important intentions, something that serves as your emotional and intellectual anchor.

You can create an icon that you physically carry around with you, say on a chain around your neck, or one whose image is always vivid in your mind. Examples of icons include the cross for observant Christians and the Star of David for observant Jews. These icons carry volumes of meaning in a simple, portable, brilliant way. Other such icons include the dove of peace, the image of the Buddha, the clenched fist of black power, and the rainbow flag of gay pride.

Rarely, however, do we create personal icons that encapsulate our individual life purposes. People tend never to do this simply because it doesn't occur to them. But it is wonderful to embody your personal life purposes and intentions in a unique icon.

First, think about your life purposes: What are they? What do you see as your meaning investments and your meaning opportunities in life? Next, begin to think about what sort of powerful symbol might capture the essence of your life purposes. Look in your mind's eye, in nature, on the internet, in books, and elsewhere. A walking stick, a polished stone, a lighthouse — what might your life-purpose icon be?

Once you've chosen your icon, think about how you will employ it and carry it with you. Will you make a representation of it yourself? Will you ask a jewelry maker to fabricate it for you? Will you display it on your phone or computer screen? Think about how to make your chosen life-purpose icon always available to you.

Food for Thought

Here are a few questions that will help you determine whether you grew up in a sad or anxious family, whether you are in one currently, and, if either is true, what you want to do about that now. Engaging with these questions will help you become better aware of your own situation. That awareness may open the door to important changes that you might make to reduce your sadness or anxiety or to handle other challenges.

1. To what extent was your family of origin a sad or anxious family?

2. If your family of origin was a sad or anxious family, what were the consequences for you?

3. To what extent is your current family a sad or anxious family?

4. If you currently live in a sad or anxious family, how can you use your tool kit to deal more effectively with the challenges you're facing?

CHAPTER TEN

Loveless and Distant Families

Love is not a given in family life. We've mythologized love to such an extent that we have come to believe that it is the natural state between mates, between parents and their children, and between siblings. We've done this even though we don't see much love — or related states like warmth, kindness, affection, and closeness — in real life.

What we more often see are announcements and protestations of love, coupled with a colder, angrier, or more disinterested reality. "I love my mother, but I don't like anything about her." "I love my brother, but I want to kill him most of the time." "My father always says that he loves me, but he can't seem to find any time to spend with me, and he wants to get away almost the second he sees me." "I love my son, but we haven't talked in six months." If asked, family members feel obliged to say that they love one another; but are they acting in loving, close ways?

Genuinely loving relationships among family members are

probably relatively rare. Even spouses who like each other well enough and who remain committed to each other may have had the flame of passion die out and may be too overwhelmed by life to be able to show much affection to each other or to anyone else. Life doesn't seem to do much to help support our loving feelings.

This lack of love matters. Disinterest harms us. Distance harms us. A lack of love harms us. There are few feelings worse than feeling that we grew up unloved, and the consequences of that experience include hollow feelings, a lack of self-worth, simmering anger at the unfairness of life, self-destructive tendencies, and severe difficulty in loving, maybe verging on an inability to love. Whether that lack of love happened in our family of origin or is happening now, its effects are real.

Some of the results of family coldness are at first glance surprising — but not at second glance. It may seem initially surprising that a seemingly cold man or woman should be having a secret, tempestuous affair. But of course these extramarital affairs make perfect sense. Many of the dynamics inside the difficult families we're discussing promote extramarital affairs, and a loveless and distant marriage is an excellent source of such dynamics.

It's common for an apparently distant and nonsexual couple to deal with the lack of warmth and love in their marriage by secretly engaging in torrid affairs. The family therapy researchers Jeanfreau, Jurich, and Mong observe:

> From 33–75% of men to 26–70% of women have been involved in an extramarital relationship. In research studies, prior to becoming involved in an extramarital relationship the women all expressed the inability

to resolve conflict within their marriages. The women described wanting to have a stronger connection with their husbands, whether it was by being shown more attention, physical affection, or simply by spending more time talking. According to the participants' perceptions, their husbands did not reciprocate the same level of desire the women were having for the stronger connection within their marriages.

Whether it's the wife who's not getting enough from the marriage, the husband, or both, results like affairs are to be expected. So are results like children acting out as a means of forcing their parents to notice them and deal with them, and estrangements that seem to arise because of some difference of opinion over religion, sexual orientation, politics, or career path but are really about long-term coldness, indifference, and a lack of love.

Being Yourself in a Loveless or Distant Family

What can you do if you find yourself in this situation? Use your tool kit in the following ways and in additional ways that you dream up.

- *Be smart.* Maybe love can't be manufactured. But you can smartly work to grow closer to family members by seeking each one out individually and having small, private, heartfelt conversations. Pull your sister aside and ask her how her life is going. Come from the place of genuinely wanting to know. If it is smart to accept that you can't make love happen by snapping your fingers, it is also smart to assume that you may be able to create more closeness.

If you're trapped in a loveless and distant family, another smart thing to do is to foster relationships outside the family. Your relationship needs are unlikely to be met in a family whose members keep their distance. At the same time, you want to be careful that your need for closeness does not cause you to jump too deeply into other relationships. Because you have a strong need for closeness, you're at risk of seeking it in relationships that don't serve you or even hurt you, like marrying or becoming pregnant too early, which can dramatically change the course of your journey. Closeness is great, but losing yourself or giving yourself away is not. Being smart means valuing both real closeness and strong boundaries.

- *Be strong.* Love requires real strength of character: it demands that we stand vulnerable, patient, and open. Falling into line with the rest of your family and living a closed, defended, unapproachable life may be easier than opening up, letting down your defenses, and expressing your feelings, when you know that you risk meeting with a cold reception, silence, and rejection. But isn't the payoff of actual closeness and some genuine fellow feeling worth that risk?

- *Be calm.* We crave a loving reaction from our so-called loved ones. When we get coldness, scorn, criticism, indifference, or dismissal instead, we're likely to experience a strong negative reaction that can cause us to grow agitated, lose our balance, and react impulsively or destructively. Being calm in such situations means knowing how to dial down that agitation so that you don't lash out, burn bridges, or self-destruct. Rehearse

what you will do to keep calm and maintain (or re-
gain) your composure when you're scorned, dismissed,
or frozen out.

- *Be clear.* Stay clear on the value of love and closeness,
even if they are in terribly short supply in your family. By staying clear about their importance, you build
your determination to find them somewhere. Your
family may act as though being cold and distant is exactly the way to be, but don't buy it. A lack of love is not
some sort of guiding principle — it's heartbreaking.

- *Be aware.* Are there openings for contact with family
members, even just brief ones? Are there moments of
affection that you might build on? Are there things to
like about family members that, if you acknowledged
them, might lead to new closeness? By staying aware of
the possibilities for love and closeness that may exist in
your family, you give yourself the best chance possible
to change family dynamics and get your needs met.

- *Be brave.* It takes courage to say to your son, "You seem
so far away all the time. Can't we just visit and chat?"
It takes courage to say to your father, "You never say
you love me or even that you like me. Is it that you
don't feel affection for me, or is it that you just have
trouble expressing it?" It takes courage to say to your
older brother, "I know you're a lot older than me and
have your own life, but can't we be a little closer?" Take
a deep breath and muster the courage to say what you
feel and to ask for what you want.

- *Be present.* Say that something your parents do feels like
an expression of hatred for you. Maybe they've cut you
out of their will; maybe they're paying for college for

their other children but not for you. Can you even be around them after that? Yes, if you hold being around them as an opportunity to practice presence, to learn how to "be" in situations that disturb you and where you usually act out or leave. Monks have the luxury of practicing presence in the quiet of a dedicated meditation space. You must practice presence in the middle of taxing and emotional real-life situations!

- *Be resilient.* If you grew up in a loveless and distant family, you may find yourself expressing those same unfortunate qualities. You would be thrilled to allow yourself to feel closer to your loved ones, but it's a battle to let down your guard and open up your heart. What's required is the everyday resilience to persist in your efforts at love and closeness in the face of your own formed personality. If you failed at love and closeness today, manifest your resilience and try for love and closeness tomorrow!

Compassion Training for Parents

Studies have shown what we all intuitively know: that when parents feel compassion and love for their children, they feel less stress in their presence and react to children's problematic behavior less harshly and punitively. According to one parenting study:

Compassionate love appeared to help mothers, and particularly those who experienced strong physiological arousal during difficult parenting situations, establish positive socialization contexts for their children and avoid stress-induced adverse parenting. Adopting a stance of acceptance and compassion toward one's child may help mothers focus on providing parental support rather than reacting to their own heightened physiological arousal. Despite being physiologically stressed, the caring humanism and other-focused goals that underlie a compassionate orientation to caregiving provided mothers with resources they could draw on to avoid resorting to a fight-or-flight style of harsh parenting.

For financial reasons, a client of mine, Matthew, found himself living with his pregnant wife in his parents' home. He characterized that household as "the land of the living dead." No matter who was home, the house always felt cold and empty. His father and mother each had a way of leaving the room the moment someone else entered it, as did his two sullen — everyone called them "quiet" — brothers. It was almost like some sort of joke.

Matthew knew that his family's style had something to do with his parents' experiences in their country of origin and as penniless immigrants to America. His father, a violin teacher, had apparently been a political activist in the Balkans, and his activism had led to harsh consequences — but no one talked about that. The silence and secrecy around the past only intensified the pervasive sense of distance that Matthew felt.

We talked about the imminent birth of his first child and his worries that he and his wife would somehow not love their newborn. One sort of answer to such a worry is to smile and exclaim, "Of course you will!" But that response is hardly enough, given that many new parents do not, in fact, bond well with their newborns, or even seem able to take a genuine interest in them. I asked Matthew to research what concrete steps he might take to prepare himself to be a loving parent.

One day he came in and announced that he'd discovered that a class on compassion training for new parents was being offered at his local Jewish Community Center. Did I think attending it might be a good idea? I handed him back the question: Did he think it might be a good idea? He instantly replied that he thought that it would, for his wife as well as for him. He quietly observed that his wife had a loveless streak in her, just as he had, and that it probably arose from the same source, her own cold and loveless childhood. They could both use some compassion training.

Although Matthew wanted to attend the class, his wife balked. She felt insulted: Did he really believe that she wouldn't love her own child? He couldn't make himself say, "Yes, I think that's possible." He presumed, maybe rightly so, that such a charge, once voiced, might never be forgiven. So instead he said, "How could it hurt?" His wife made other protestations, about her tiredness, about how many things remained to be done before the baby arrived, and so on; but finally she agreed.

A few days after the first class, I asked Matthew how it had gone. "Pretty emotionally and pretty spectacularly," he replied. "We were completely unprepared for how emotional we both got. Neither of us ever cries…and we both wept. I'm not sure why exactly the floodgates opened. I think the only way to say it is that something in us thawed. My wife had an even bigger reaction than I did."

But the next time we met, Matthew was sad again. "Whatever we gained from that class and the subsequent ones," he said, "only made living at my parents' house feel worse. It was like, now that we see what love feels like, the lack of love in that house felt truly terrible. We both felt a kind of rage and wanted to confront my parents and shout something or other at them. But of course we didn't; and stopping ourselves from speaking — stopping ourselves from coming from the heart — only made living there feel that much worse. I don't think we can stay there!"

We strategized about how they could move out. It came down to a simple question: Was living rent-free and having a lot of space worth living in an empty, loveless, and cold environment, or would renting a tiny, cramped place of their own be the better bet? It is always hard to weigh a financial good against an emotional good: How many mates stay in marriages long after they want to leave because they fear becoming suddenly poor? These are among our hardest and most consequential decisions. The baby arrived, and still Matthew and his wife hadn't decided. Or rather, by doing nothing, they had made their decision.

Then one day Matthew came and said, "We've moved." He seemed very happy. I asked him what had led to the change. He replied, "It happened one evening. The baby was crying. My wife was in the other room, and before she had a chance to get to him, my mother walked by the baby's crib, made a face — I'm not sure you'd exactly call it disgust, but disgust is close enough — and then looked at me, as much as to say, 'Can you please take care of this?' It was almost as if her look said, 'Can't you take care of this monstrosity?' That was it. I went out the very next day and found us a place, and we moved within the week."

I wondered aloud about what sort of relationship he wanted to maintain with his parents. Matthew shook his head. "I don't know," he replied. "But I'm convinced that what they do — that who they are — is infectious. I refuse to have our baby infected. I don't think that exactly means that I'm going to prevent them from seeing him — as if they want to! — but it does mean something. I don't know what yet. Maybe I'll only let them visit if they pledge to smile! That's a joke — no, I don't know what relationship I mean to maintain with them. I only know that I can't let their frigidity harm our baby."

CEREMONY: Becoming a Past Whisperer

Let's say that you were unloved growing up. You have worked on your mental health by getting a grip on your thoughts, by engaging in healing rituals and ceremonies, by reaching out to people, by relating, and in many other ways. But that good work feels threatened by the way that the past keeps intruding upon the present. Bad feelings just keep coming back.

Remembering and reexperiencing the past can make us panic and despair, and it can derail us in all sorts of ways. Encountering the past in our formed personality, seeing the way we are now because of what happened back then, can confound us and sabotage us. Unfortunately, the present inevitably contains the past.

Even if we are mindful and train ourselves not to think thoughts that subvert us, even if we do a beautiful job of cognitive self-awareness and a fantastic job of pursuing our life purposes, that cruel rebuke that we received thirty years ago is still stinging our cheeks. Our embarrassed moments from forty years ago or fifty years ago still circulate somewhere in our blood. That is how we are built. The past is here with us, and we must deal with it.

To help you quiet a past that is still storming through your system, try to become a past whisperer. Mindfully face the past and settle it down, just as a horse whisperer calms a wild, powerful horse. You turn to the past, whether that past is fifty years ago and dusty or only a moment ago and still electric, and you say, "Be easy, past."

Try one of the following ceremonies. Get a bowl and sprinkle a little water into the bowl. As you sprinkle the water, say, "Be easy, past." Or light a candle and say, "Be easy, past." watch the candle flicker, and repeat your mantra. You can test yourself by looking at photos of your childhood while saying, "Be easy, past." Or practice saying, "Be easy, past," before a family gathering like Thanksgiving dinner. Today, spend a little time picturing yourself as a past whisperer. Create a ceremony that supports your intention to become skillful at calming the past that still circulates within you.

Many difficult families present in-your-face challenges like bullying, chaos, or alcoholism. Some present subtler challenges, challenges that are felt but often never quite named. Loveless and distant families produce challenges of this sort. You feel the painful lack of love and the heartbreaking distance between family members, but you may not have a name for what you're experiencing. I hope that this chapter has helped you to name this problem — and given you a sense of how you can use your tool kit to deal with it.

Food for Thought

1. To what extent was your family of origin a loveless or distant family?

2. If your family of origin was a loveless or distant family, what were the consequences for you?

3. To what extent is your current family a loveless or distant family?

4. If you currently inhabit a loveless or distant family, how can you make use of your tool kit to more effectively deal with the challenges you're facing?

CHAPTER ELEVEN

Warring and Divided Families

Many families are divided and at war. The most typical division is between a battling husband and wife. That warfare regularly leads to divorce, and it may continue long after the divorce has been finalized.

Family divisions can come in many forms:

- Two siblings may start out battling as young children and stay at war their whole lives.
- The war may be between two sides of the family, a Hatfield and McCoy situation, where each side holds some major grievance against the other. Extended-family events, like weddings and funerals, are marked by tantrums and tears.
- Classic wars flare up between women and their mothers-in-law, between teenagers and parents, and between parents and adult children who return home after a divorce or a job loss.

These wars, as our daily headlines shout, sometimes end tragically. They affect everyone in the family, including those who try to stay out of the line of fire. And there are often life-long consequences. According to one team of researchers:

> Children whose parents divorce are more likely to see their own marriages end in divorce, and these children are also more likely to report relationship problems, conflict, perceived instability, and lack of trust in their own relationships. This body of research also indicates that problems in the parents' marriage involving jealousy, anger, overly critical behavior, poor spousal communication, and a tendency for one spouse to dominate the other all appear to have negative effects on offspring's future marriages. The quality of the parents' marriage in many ways sets the family climate for marital partners and children alike, and has been shown to have far reaching influences on offspring in later romantic relationships.

Often these wars play themselves out most loudly and poignantly as parents age and their children are obliged to help out. Twyla Hill writes:

> Children, particularly daughters, provide much of the family care that is done for elderly people. The typical adult child caregiver is a married daughter between the ages of 45 and 64 years old. Typically, she aids her parent for over four years and provides assistance seven days a week with no help from anyone else. Limitations on the caregiver's life because of caregiving (such as less time

with friends or other family members), the caregiver's perception of overload, and whether or not respite care is available also impact the amount of burden caregivers feel. Sibling relationships also can be sources of stress, as sisters and brothers may disagree about what should be done, who should provide care, and if the help being given is acceptable.

Sometimes the wars that erupt are situational — for example, when a teenager's first choice of college flies in the face of what one or both parents want. Just as often, the wars and divisions are long-standing and always simmering away — for example, when one mate holds a strong grudge against the other for not earning enough, spending profligately, never honoring promises, and so on. We might focus on any of these areas, but let's pay some special attention to the ways that siblings fight and what you can do if you find yourself in that particular line of fire.

Siblings Divided

The pretty picture of brotherly and sisterly love is belied by what we see in real families. Siblings are easily disaffected — and they very often stay disaffected. It is common for brothers and sisters to fall out, for early alliances and divisions to last a lifetime, for grudges to be held, and for public feuds to erupt. Sibling relationships can be both fragile and volatile.

One starting place for all this disaffection has to do with siblings' perceived pecking order. Jeanne Safer explains: "Rivalry, competition and anxiety about your place in your parents' affections... [can breed] rancor that haunts siblings all their lives and occurs in each phase of adulthood — work, marriage, parenthood, caring for aging parents, and eventually, settling that perpetual minefield, the estate."

These disaffections, rivalries, competitions, and bad blood can bother siblings deeply and even cause illness. One team of therapists observes: "Although the amount of sibling contact diminishes as children age and move out of their parents' homes, sibling relationships continue to influence adult well-being. Indeed, the quality of sibling relationships is one of the most important long-term predictors of mental health in old age."

The seeds of lifelong disturbance and distress are planted in childhood: who got the better presents, who got away with more, who was esteemed and who was mocked, who bullied whom, who was beaten and who was spared beatings, who was considered beautiful and who plain, and countless other everyday dynamics leading to feelings of envy, anger, and even hatred.

Some of these dynamics are straightforward. If you perceive your brother or sister as mean to you or dismissive of you, for example, or if you believe your brother or sister holds you in contempt, it's easy to see where the rancor comes from. But other dynamics, like coalitions and allegiances, can be more subtle and complicated. For example, you may not like your younger brother, but you may nevertheless align yourself with him because he is favored in the family. You may unconsciously be looking for some of that favoritism to rub off on you, or maybe the safest place in your family is in the vicinity of a favored sibling.

Underlying so many of these difficult dynamics are perceptions and questions of fairness (or, as social scientists put it, questions of equity). If you feel that your sibling is being treated better than you are, you are likely to feel angry and upset. If you feel that your sibling is not treating you fairly and equitably, that too is likely to provoke rancor. Equity theorists who have closely examined sibling relationships conclude that a felt sense of inequity can lead to lifelong ruptures and to countless practical disagreements, including lawsuits.

The researchers Whiteman, McHale, and Soli explain: "The provision of care for a parent usually falls on the shoulders of one offspring, and primary caregivers often report feelings of distress when their siblings fail to share caregiving responsibilities. When efforts to create equity were unsuccessful, distress increased. In fact, one study showed that when caregiving inequities were too great, sibling relationship dissolution occurred. Researchers found that siblings stopped interacting or even sought legal action against one another when distress over caregiving became intense."

Being Smart in Dealing with Siblings

Here are ten tips to help you deal with your siblings in a way that is safer, more effective, and smarter:

- *Accept that there is a dark side to sibling relationships.* You may be envied for being favored, you may hate your siblings because they were better treated than you, you may hold some grudge over a minor matter — that favorite toy that got destroyed — or over a major one — for example, sexual abuse by a sibling. It isn't possible to paste a pretty face onto sibling relationships and make believe that all is sweetness and light.
- *See which old perceptions need updating.* Maybe you've been resentful for decades that your younger sister was entitled, got away with murder, was praised when she

didn't deserve praise, and had too much handed to her. Even if that was all true, do you need to still see her that way now that she has two divorces behind her and serious health problems? Is it time to forgive her and update your mental picture of her? The issue is not whether you should condone that past unfairness but whether you may want to see her as she is today and not as she was when she was five or twelve or seventeen. She has been through the wringer now, too, hasn't she?

- *Be safe.* It isn't okay for one of your siblings to harm you physically or emotionally. If you're living with your family of origin, go to your parents, even if you're convinced that they won't take your side. Don't stop there. Go to a trusted adult and reveal what's happening. Check out online resources that provide information, hotlines, reporting instructions, and other vital help. There are books that may help, among them Vernon Wiehe, *What Parents Need to Know about Sibling Abuse: Breaking the Cycle of Violence*; Richard J. Gelles and Suzanne K. Steinmetz, *Behind Closed Doors: Violence in the American Family*; and John Caffaro and Allison Conn-Caffaro, *Sibling Abuse Trauma: Assessment and Intervention Strategies for Children, Families and Adults.* Violence against you is not okay!

- *Have a conversation in a different setting.* If it is important to you to forge a better relationship with a sibling, create a chance for that to happen. You may feel that you might be able to mend your fences with a brother or sister, but the opportunity for a real heart-to-heart chat never seems to arise, certainly not at the annual (painful) Thanksgiving dinner or in the midst of your everyday lives. You might suggest a weekend away or even just a walk by the lake or the ocean. Who knows: one honest, heartfelt conversation might completely alter your relationship for the better. Of course, it might not: but if your intuition tells you that such a conversation is worth the risk, make it happen.

- *Be clear.* Families often maintain secrets, create false scenarios, and perpetuate lies. You may be holding something against your brother or your sister that never actually happened or that happened quite differently from the way the family tells the story. Maybe you don't know the whole story about what happened. Maybe your brother did act out — but not until your father started punishing him cruelly. Wouldn't that second part of the story be important to know? Maybe your sister did have an abortion — but for reasons that put her actions in a very different light. Two questions that naturally arise are, "Who knows the truth?" and, "Will they tell it to you?" Is one family member the most objective and the most reliable truth teller? You might approach that person and finally get the real story.

- *Detach from alliances.* Ever since childhood you may have aligned with one sibling to gang up on another: perhaps you talked behind your older sister's back and in other ways created an "us against her" alliance. Think about whether you want to perpetuate that alliance. Maybe you never really felt good about it; maybe you've secretly wanted to improve your relationship with the disavowed sibling for the longest time. Is this the moment to do exactly that?

- *Close the distance.* Maybe distance opened up over time between you and your sibling because one of you had children and the other didn't, because of geographical distance, or for some other reason. Maybe the distance was there from the beginning, maybe because your sibling came into your life when a parent remarried or because he or she was half a generation younger or older than you. Maybe you've grown apart and have very different lives and very different interests. Do you want to close that distance a bit? Is this a moment for some new closeness? If it is, what would be required to make closing that gap happen?

- *Let go of grudges.* Was it really your brother's fault that your parents gave him far more money for college than they gave you? (Wasn't that really much more your parents' doing?) Was it really your sister's fault that she won awards that you coveted? (Should she really have performed poorly just for your sake?) Are there some grudges that it makes sense to let go of now, either for the sake of an improved relationship with your sibling or just to lighten your load of grudges?

- *Envision a different relationship.* How would you like to see your relationship with a brother or sister change and improve? If you can get a picture of that — maybe it involves spending more time together, maybe it has to do with sharing more deeply, maybe it requires that you take a strong stance with respect to some problematic behavior, like drinking or stealing — then think through what concrete actions you might take in the service of that vision. Once you name those actions,

see if you want to muster your courage and enact
them.

- *Choose for today.* How do you want to be with your
brother or sister today? Maybe today is a day to avoid
your brother. Maybe today is a day to reconcile. Maybe
today is a day to have a simple, shared moment with your
sister: a meal, a movie, or a board game. Maybe today is
a day to have an important conversation. Maybe today
is a day to be helpful, loving, and kind. Maybe today is a
day to speak up, be brave, and say what you need to say.

Many of my clients live in a perpetual war zone, embroiled
in years of conflict with an ex-husband who is always taking
them to court, a sibling who repeatedly levels the same charges
from the distant past, or an adult child repeatedly unburdening
himself of his grievances. Few things are more taxing, stressful,
or harmful to your physical and mental health than these never-
ending battles.

One of my clients could not find a way to end the battle with her ex-husband's father, except by capitulating to his
demands about his son's rights regarding the couple's two
children. She wanted freedom from the battle, but not at the
expense of giving in and harming the children.

The father-in-law always seemed to have some new threat
up his sleeve: a new way to reduce child support, a new charge
to make in court about her fitness. That my client had not become seriously ill during this long siege and relentless series of
threats was something of a miracle. What actually helped was
using her tool kit.

With my help, she learned to ask herself what was the
smart thing to do when a new attack came, rather than responding emotionally. She had practiced speaking strongly,

and that skill now came naturally to her. She had ways of calming herself when the onslaught came, such as using her garden as a sanctuary and using incantations to calm herself (the one she particularly liked was "I trust my resources"). She had learned to ask for clarification when she didn't understand one of her father-in-law's demands, a response that often caused him to back down somewhat. She had acquired, practiced, and learned skills that allowed her to deal as best as she could with a bad situation, one that was not going away anytime soon. And, really, what more can we ask of ourselves?

Three Ceremonies

Finding the Safety of the Castle: You live in a land regularly threatened by invaders. When the invaders approach, you withdraw to the protection of the castle, where you and your family will be safe. Invaders have never breached those castle walls in a thousand years. It is anything but an ideal situation, but people inside the castle walls still fall in love, raise children, create art, make friends, and live. Picture yourself in that safe castle. Yes, you are under siege. Yes, you are praying for the invaders to leave. But at the same time, you are safe, and you can live. Picture yourself living, breathing, and even smiling within the castle walls. To finish the ceremony, make yourself a cup of tea and enjoy it within the safety of those walls.

Making a Peace Offering: Maybe the war between you and another family member has run its course, and a truce is now possible. Or maybe you have the feeling that some small gesture or effort might change the dynamic between you and a family member with whom you're feuding. In that case, enact a peace-offering ceremony. Text or email the family member and see if he or she is willing to meet. At the appointed time, arrive with your peace offering — say, a pizza that you both like. Say, "I've brought us a pizza to share as a peace offering. I wonder if there's a way we can make peace? Do you think there might be a chance?" Lead with compassion, goodwill, and genuine hope for a truce.

Narrowing the Gap: Maybe your family is divided along some fault line. Maybe you are trying to remain neutral, or maybe you've chosen a side. You know that the tensions between the two sides are terrible and that you'd love to do something to bring the warring sides together and arrange a truce. You might begin by engaging in the following visualization.

Picture the two sides separated by a gap, like the gap between the train and the platform in a London Underground station. The gap may be deep, but it isn't all that wide. Ask yourself, "What might narrow that gap?" Relax, breathe, wait, and see if an answer comes to you. If it does, translate it into an action step, and see if you want to commit to taking that action. If no answer comes, ask yourself, "Okay, if the gap can't be narrowed, is there a way to just step right over it?" Again relax, breathe, wait, and see if anything comes to you. Whether or not you get some useful answer to either question, end the ceremony by honoring and celebrating your effort to improve the quality of your family's life.

If you're living in a divided or warring family, you know how taxing those battles and onslaughts feel. Hardly anything feels worse than having to defend yourself against a family member's attacks or having to take a side in some horrible feud. There are few good answers as to how to resolve such conflicts, just as there are few good answers to the horrors of war. But you can use your tool kit to think about how to reduce the level of conflict, help yourself heal from inevitable wounds, and make yourself as safe as possible. Just as there will always be wars and divisions among nations, there will always be warring and divided families. Use your tool kit to survive yours.

Food for Thought

1. To what extent was your family of origin a warring and divided family?
2. If your family of origin was a warring and divided family, what were the consequences for you?
3. To what extent is your current family a warring and divided family?
4. If you currently inhabit a warring and divided family, how can you use your tool kit to deal more effectively with the challenges you're facing?

CHAPTER TWELVE

Bullying, Aggressive, and Abusive Families

Some families are characterized by their bullying, aggressive, or abusive nature. Sometimes this behavior rises to the level of criminality; but even when it does not, it is always cruel and harmful. Worse still, these cruelties are infectious. A father bullies his oldest son; that son, who ought to know better given that he understands how terrible it feels to be bullied, turns around and bullies his younger brother. Being harmed ourselves seems to teach us to harm others, rather than teaching us not to harm. What an unfortunate feature of human nature!

Frequently an older sibling bullies a younger sibling. Maya, a client of mine who is now in her forties, still felt bullied in every interaction with her older brothers, who made all family financial decisions and ruled with an iron hand. Although they never struck her in adulthood as they had done when she was a child, she always felt physically threatened in their presence and believed that any of them would gladly strike her if she ever stood up to them.

Bullying and aggression can take various forms. One partner may bully or physically intimidate the other. A parent may act aggressively and abusively toward a child. A grandparent may physically abuse and bully a grandchild. A teenager may act out violently toward his parents.

This last dynamic may sound surprising, but often it's the teenage children in the family who are the bullies, abusers, or aggressors. Child-on-parent violence, while much less well known than parent-on-child violence, happens all too frequently. When I interviewed Laurie Reid, a licensed marriage and family therapist who operates Breaking the Cycle Consulting, she observed:

> One important key to understanding child-to-parent abuse is to know that it is certainly not a phase. This form of domestic violence…is defined as any harmful and demeaning behaviors by a child that cause physical, psychological, or financial distress to a parent or caregiver.…Parents often feel embarrassed or helpless, not knowing where to turn, and rarely report violence for fear of being judged. It's not uncommon for parents to downplay the seriousness of the abuse in order to avoid public and social-system scrutiny.…Most parents often think when their child lashes out that they are just being children and the phase will soon pass over.…But when these actions turn into abuse, it is no longer a small problem but a large one that needs to be addressed immediately.

Maybe what's going on in your family hasn't risen to this level but is more in the category of bullying. If you're a parent and your family life is being made toxic by the bullying behaviors of your children, here is a summary of tips provided by Sherri Gordon at Verywell.com:

- *Don't ignore sibling aggression.* While it is normal for siblings to argue and tease one another, chronic mean behavior, verbal and physical, should never be ignored.
- *Get to know your child's friends.* Your children's friends often have a huge influence on their behavior, and peer pressure is a very strong force when it comes to bullying.
- *Talk with your kids about bullying.* Be sure your children know that life is full of disagreements and that hitting, name-calling, and blaming are never the answers.
- *Foster empathy.* Work with your children to recognize how their behavior affects others. Be sure to ask your child how he would feel in a similar situation.
- *Put an end to bullying behavior immediately.* If you find your child is a bully or a cyberbully, take steps to put an end to the behavior at once. Be sure you take swift action with appropriate consequences.

Consider the situation of my client Joan. Over the previous year something profoundly dark had begun to happen in Joan's life. Her husband, a successful doctor, had bullied her constantly from the time they first met. His personality horrified her, he hated and derided his patients, and she blanched whenever he insulted her, her family, or their friends. Still, she had learned to live with his cruelty. What was new was how her twin sons, now eleven years old, were beginning to take after their father.

They were becoming little monsters. They mocked her, they refused to listen to her, they repeated their father's insults, and they teamed up with their father, making a gang of three. Joan begged them to stop: they laughed at her. When she tried to explain to her parents what was going on, they refused to listen. Her husband found her concerns ridiculous and sided with the boys. It felt too difficult and shameful to share her feelings and her concerns with other members of her family, even though she had a good relationship with her two sisters. She had no clue what to do.

She explained all of this to me. I asked her to think about how she might use her tool kit. Two ideas came to her. First, she believed that if she could be more present in the moment — more of a presence, so to speak — the boys would be less likely to bully her. Second, she wondered if she could express herself more clearly, with less hesitation and fewer apologies. I asked her to translate these two ideas into concrete actions. She came up with two actions. She resolved that when the boys bullied her, first she would say nothing, and by saying nothing, staying put, and staring them down, she would make her presence felt; and once they felt her presence, she would say, "Never say that to me again."

We agreed that she would need her strength and her courage to pull this off. She committed to trying out her experiment in being present and to reporting the results. Three days later I received an email from her. Joan wrote:

> I did it. The boys were mocking me about how I made their sandwiches at lunch. I stopped making their sandwiches, stood there, and stared at them. At first they just laughed and went on mocking me. Then their laughter got a little more nervous, and finally Adam said, "What's

going on, Mom?" Then I said, very slowly and I think very powerfully, "Never say that to me again." They just stared at me. But I think something shifted. They've been quieter…and less mean…I don't know, I think that something good may have happened.

When Children Are the Victims

Of course, more often the children are the abused and the adults are the abusers. How do children try to protect themselves in an abusive family? According to the researchers Carbonell, Reinherz, and Beardslee, the two primary methods children employ are "planful evasion" and "seeking and activating support":

While previous research has identified avoidance as a coping strategy often employed during times of adversity (with limited effectiveness), what we heard our respondents describe was qualitatively different. They did not describe themselves as passive, nor in denial of the circumstances that made their lives difficult. Instead, they talked about the evasion of adversity, most often when they were quite young, as an active and planful strategy for protecting themselves from harm. Respondents who used evasion of adversity described developing strategies for physically avoiding violent people or situations. Respondents also stressed the importance of social support in their lives. Seeking out other people and asking for help offered an avenue to find ways of coping that the participants may not have found alone.

Be Clear: Who's Your Ally?

Here's the advice I give to children and young adults who experience violence within the family. If you're experiencing bullying, aggression, or abuse, make an ally — in your own family, if you can. Is there someone in your extended family who understands that you are being bullied and who sees that as not okay? That someone might be a grandparent, an aunt or uncle, or a cousin — technology being what it is, it's easy to stay in touch with your ally even if he or she lives halfway around the world. This person might become a confidante, someone you can talk to so that your feelings don't get bottled up and your experiences don't go unreported.

But an ally is more than just a confidante: it is someone with whom you plan and who may be in a position to intervene or help in some other way. Make a list of everyone in the family, no matter how old or young or how geographically close or distant, and mark your ally candidates with a star. Reach out to one of them and say, "I need to tell you something. May I?" If that relationship doesn't pan out — if that person doesn't seem interested enough or sympathetic enough — try the next candidate on your list. Try making at least one ally!

Try to make allies outside your family as well. You can't have too many! You might reach out to a teacher, a school counselor, a coach, a Sunday school teacher, or a professional like a social worker whose job it is to protect you. Of course it's scary to reach out, to reveal family secrets, and to perhaps start a process that may ultimately involve social services and the criminal justice system; it might cause huge disruptions and changes in your life. But if you're being harmed, you must consider reaching out and looking for allies as one of your options.

A teenager in this predicament would also profit from being smart and thinking ahead. As Marie Hartwell-Walker advises:

> It may not be fair, but it's important to be real. Unloving parents aren't going to prepare you for independence. They're just going to be glad when you move out. It falls on you to learn the skills you need to know to survive out there on your own. Make a list of what you need to know how to do, from doing your own laundry to managing money, and set out to learn how to do it. Get a job and start putting money away so you can rent a place of your own the day you graduate from high school. Get good grades and ask your school counselor to help you identify scholarships so you can go away to college.

Being Smart in a Bullying, Aggressive, or Abusive Family

You must have your wits about you to survive a bullying, aggressive, or abusive family. Here are some smart things to do:

- Is your father particularly hostile and aggressive when he arrives home from work but mellower (or just sleepier) later in the evening? If so, it would be smart to avoid him when he first gets home.
- Is your sister especially abusive when she hears that you've had a success at school? Then it would be smart not to share your school successes with her.
- Are alcohol or drugs part of the problem? Then it would be smart to learn about twelve-step programs geared to helping families of people abusing alcohol or drugs, and consider attending meetings.
- Do you like to taunt the bully in your family? Does that

actually work for you? If it doesn't, then it would be smart to stop those taunting behaviors.

- Is the aggressor someone who only visits occasionally, like an uncle or a grandparent? Do you get some warning that he or she is coming? Then it would be smart to make sure to be away or safely in your room when he or she visits.
- Does that bullying adult tend to arrive unexpectedly? Then it would be smart to figure out ways of leaving the house as quickly as possible or getting yourself to the safety of a locked room when he or she suddenly appears.
- Given that you know how your family operates, it would be smart of you to use that knowledge to your advantage!

CEREMONY: Changing Sooner Rather Than Later

We are all burdened by circumstances: unrewarding work, a loveless marriage, troubles afflicting those we love, threats from the world, or thwarted hopes and dreams. Or maybe they're circumstances of the sort we've been discussing in this chapter — living in a bullying, aggressive, or abusive family. These circumstances harm our emotional health.

Often these circumstances can't be changed easily. In fact, it is common for folks who know that they really must make a change to take five or six years to make it. Sometimes the change never happens, and the pain persists. When we continue to live in adverse circumstances, it is easy to find life frustrating. We try to manage those frustrations as best we can, often in ways that harm us. Those tactics then become part of our circumstances: now we have not only our unrewarding job to deal with but also the excessive shopping, pornography watching, drinking, or drug taking that we use to escape the original problem.

The following ceremony can help. Imagine that there is a change you know that you need to make. Let's say it's finding an ally to support you in your efforts to end the bullying that you're experiencing. Finding that ally may be challenging and slow. One small step is to name this challenge and then to say, "Sooner rather than later."

Of course, just saying these words doesn't change your circumstances. But it keeps the intention front and center in your mind. It causes you to stand a little taller and helps you feel more equal to making the change. It signals a possibility: that maybe the change really can happen sooner rather than later. It provokes your brain to look for solutions and pay attention. It isn't the change itself, but it opens the door to changing.

Change involves risk. It's risky even to suggest to ourselves that we need to change, since we may have failed before at keeping our resolutions and so may fear disappointing ourselves again. Courage is needed. Unpack your bravery tool from your tool kit. Identify a change in circumstances that you need to make and then say, "Sooner rather than later."

Say it a few times. Let those words echo and reverberate through your system. If saying them galvanizes you to make the change, congratulations! But even if you don't manage to jump right up and initiate the change, let those four simple words create an opening that supports the shift you want. The phrase "Sooner rather than later" signals a powerful intention. Give this ceremony a try.

Food for Thought

1. To what extent was your family of origin a bullying, aggressive, or abusive family?
2. If your family of origin was a bullying, aggressive, or abusive family, what were the consequences for you?
3. To what extent is your current family a bullying, aggressive, or abusive family?
4. If you currently inhabit a bullying, aggressive, or abusive family, how can you make use of your tool kit to deal more effectively with the challenges you're facing?

CHAPTER THIRTEEN

Demanding, Critical, and Argumentative Families

Family members can demand a lot of one another, do a lot of criticizing, and engage in endless arguments. The 50 percent of marriages that end in divorce are regularly preceded by mutual criticism, high-pitched demands, and relentless disagreements. Arguments erupt at every stage of the life cycle: between a parent and a two-year-old, teenager, or adult child, or between an adult child and an aging parent. If you were raised in a demanding, critical, or argumentative family, or if you find yourself in one now, you know how taxing that is!

One common demand nowadays is that a child perform at the highest possible level and constantly aim for high achievement. The upside to this pressure, which is often accompanied by subtle or stinging criticism and endless commands ("Practice your violin!"), is a high likelihood that the child will indeed be successful. The downside is that the child may be emotionally harmed.

This pressure to perform, excel, and succeed may produce

a child who achieves material success. But it can also create a kind of magnetic pull toward failure. Given all that pressure to succeed, a child may only want to fail! Indeed, a child under such pressures may begin to obsess about failure.

The novelist Howard Jacobson describes this state of mind:

> I failed birth. I kept my mother waiting, arriving not just late but at a peculiar angle. I caused her pain and disappointed my father, who didn't weep exactly but would have liked his first child to have a more relaxed attitude to existence, though this was made plain to me only gradually, after years of his entering me in talent contests whenever we went on holiday to Morecambe, or pushing me up to join other kids on stage at the end of pantomimes, or shouting "Here!" and pointing to me when magicians asked for volunteers.

Even if it's said ironically, imagine believing that you failed birth!

Jackson's Fighting Family

Jackson, a young client of mine, was the second-youngest of six children growing up in a loud, tense household. Everyone yelled and screamed; even passing the peas and potatoes at dinner could cause such a ruckus that something would break or someone would get hit.

The standard volume of communication was a shout, and everyone seemed always to be holding a grudge against someone else in the family. Gender didn't enter into it: his mother and sister were as loud as his father and brothers. A few times matters got so far out of hand that the neighbors called the police.

Embarrassed by his family's behavior and desperate to stay out of the line of fire, Jackson more or less lived with his headphones on to block out the noise. But someone was always pulling his headphones off his head: his mother to yell at him for not keeping his room shipshape, his father to yell at him for some grievance now weeks or months old, his older sister to yell at him for not taking her side at dinner, his older brother first to smack him and then to yell at him for embarrassing the brother at school by his choice of clothes.

Jackson suffered from stomachaches and headaches; he couldn't keep weight on; and while he didn't quite have a name for what he was feeling, it was clearly despair. I asked him if he could think of anything to try. He shook his head: What could he try when he didn't even have permission to lock his bedroom door? The one time he tried to wedge a chair up against the door to get some privacy, his father would have broken the door down if Jackson hadn't finally yanked the chair away. No, Jackson said, he could see absolutely nothing to try.

I wondered if there were any other family members with whom he might live — or at least take a break. There weren't. I wondered if there might be one prospective ally in the household. There wasn't. But he paused and grew thoughtful. "My oldest brother is getting out of the Marines soon and coming home. He's not all screwed up like everyone else in the family. You know…I wonder." I gave him time to think. "You know," he said, "if I invite him to room with me, and he accepts, there is nobody going to barge in on him or mess with him. No one!"

"Not even your father?" I asked.

"Not even my father," Jackson replied, smiling.

Jackson reached out via email to his brother, explained the situation, invited him to room with him, and got back the reply that his brother was willing. "It's like *Walking Tall*," Jackson said. "It's like the Rock coming home." I knew that movie and nodded.

Jackson was ecstatic. But few people have the Rock or another Marine on the afternoon train arriving to rescue them. What is everyone else supposed to do?

Be Clear and Present

Say you're in a demanding marriage. Your mate is critical of everything you do — from folding the laundry to cooking the pasta — demands that things be just so, and turns every second conversation into an argument that you can't possibly win. Given that you are not leaving this marriage — at least, not yet — how might you use your tool kit to survive this toxic relationship? One tool that you'd want to pull out regularly is clarity. Clear communication might sound like "The pasta is fine," or "Fold your own laundry." Being clear in short, powerful, declarative sentences will strengthen you — and if it angers your mate, then it will bring matters to a head.

You would also want to use your presence tool. If your husband is angry because you forgot to buy mustard when you were shopping, you could defend yourself, make excuses, blame him for making you feel so anxious that it's amazing you don't forget everything, or beg him not to make such a big deal about so trivial a transgression. But would responding in any of those ways make you feel good or lead to anything but more criticism?

Rather, this is an opportunity to be present: to be aware of your breathing, to stay calm, to remain in the moment, and, after getting nicely centered and grounded, to say, "Yes, I forgot the mustard." That's the end of the story from your point of view — and if it isn't the end of the story for him, if he feels obliged to repeat the charge and make a face and wonder at your incompetence, you just stay present and, after a healthy pause, say, "Yes, I forgot the mustard."

Having to deal constantly with a demanding, critical, or argumentative family is bound to erode your mental and physical health. You must confront that reality by influencing change in your family system if possible, by protecting yourself by avoiding toxic interactions as best you can, and by employing the valuable tools in your tool kit. Your physical and mental well-being require it.

Being Resilient in the Face of Criticism

How can you deal with criticism more effectively? Your prime strategy is to grow a thicker skin and let it bounce right off you. If your skin is very sensitive, you feel every tickle and every change in temperature. If you can grow a thicker skin — through attitude change and cognitive work — you can withstand even the rudest criticism.

Your second strategy is to avoid self-criticism. It is one thing if someone else criticizes you. It is worse if you already feel critical of yourself and if criticism from the world amplifies and exacerbates your negative appraisal of yourself. You can't control what the world says, but you can decide not to bad-mouth yourself.

There are three keys to effectively handling criticism: a dynamic key, a mindfulness key, and a holistic key. The first key is growing into the sort of person who can put criticism in its place. This is a gradual process that includes consciously breaking free of the past, noticing and eliminating patterns of thought and behavior that serve you poorly, and healing from the effects of shame, guilt, and other psychological impediments. I'm calling this the *dynamic* key because it draws on the field of psychology known as psychodynamics, which deals with childhood experiences, personality formation, and enduring psychological issues.

The second key is learning how fears, worries, doubts, and negative self-talk are generated and maintained in the mind, and engaging in practices that return your mind to your conscious control. This is the *mindfulness* key, a practice combining the insights of cognitive therapy with Eastern ways of thought. This practice involves identifying and disputing negative self-talk, learning when and how to detach, and adopting mindfulness techniques that promote centering.

The third key is understanding your life purposes and committing to living in accordance with those purposes. This is the *holistic* key. You are a whole person with strengths, desires, dreams, and goals, more than just the wounded part of you that is susceptible to the sting of criticism. Allowing criticism to deflect you from your life path amounts to spiritual or existential self-sabotage. The better you understand your life purposes, the less likely it is that you'll be damaged or derailed by criticism.

In a nutshell, you learn to deal effectively with criticism by taking charge of your personality and your mind so that you can live the life you intend to lead. As you grow in this direction, you learn to deal with criticism in new, more effective ways.

How does this work in practice? A client of mine, Steven, a world-famous musician, wanted to take his music in a new direction but didn't feel equal to dealing with the criticism he knew he would receive if he changed — criticism from the people around him, from his audience, and from media critics. He'd already grown tremendously in our work together; that was why he was daring to contemplate this break with his popular music. But this change was a new — and terrifying — edge for him.

We agreed that he really had no choice in the matter. In order to grow musically, Steven had to face his fear of the inevitable criticism, and he needed to develop new tools to deal with it. He couldn't just dash off a letter to an imaginary critic (a tactic I teach in my book *Toxic Criticism*) or add an affirmation to his self-talk vocabulary in order to prepare himself for this new adventure. He understood that he would have to transform himself into someone who stood in new relationship to the idea of criticism: someone braver, more detached, and all-around savvier than he currently felt.

Steven did the work to initiate this change. About a month later we chatted on the phone. He said he was ready to unveil his new musical ideas to his business manager and to some other close confidantes. I asked him if he could explain to me how he'd changed. He replied instantly, "My new mantra is 'I invite criticism.' And I mean it. I've come full circle from fearing it like the devil to opening the door wide. If I don't take risks, I'll die. If I do take risks, people are bound to have plenty of negative things to say. I've nailed that equation in my head."

You could hear the new strength in his voice and the new wisdom in his words.

Is this work that would be valuable for you to undertake? For example, is your family critical of your choice to be an artist? I've spent the last thirty years coaching creative and performing artists, and I know a lot about the challenges they face, including their family challenges. It's hard to make art, and it's hard to sell art — and it's all even harder if your family isn't behind you or actively undermines your efforts. Artists face this challenge all the time.

Why would a family member undermine you in this way? Maybe your mate is pressuring you to make money and contribute to the family income. Maybe your child is upset with the amount of time you spend working in the studio. Maybe a parent derides your efforts and predicts financial failure for you. These family members may well have a point, but the way they're expressing it amounts to a felt lack of support and makes it that much harder for you to feel good about your choice to make and market art.

If someone in your family is angry about and critical of your decision to be an artist (or to follow some other path that displeases them), you are stuck with a difficult and perhaps volatile situation. How can you handle it? Here are some responses that don't work that well:

- Getting angry and storming away
- Feeling hurt and diminished and shrinking away
- Defending your position with "rational" arguments, counterevidence, or anecdotes about successful artists
- Ignoring the family member and the situation
- Taking to drink, drugs, sex, shopping, or some other soothing substance or activity
- Responding with countercharges of your own about other family members' choices
- Demanding support because family members "ought to" be loyal and supportive

Instead you can use all of your new skills — you can be smart, strong, calm, clear, aware, brave, present, and resilient — by saying something like this:

I agree that most artists do not make a living wage. Here are the things I am endeavoring to do to be an exception to that rule. [List your intended actions.] These efforts will take time to bear fruit, and I hope that in x amount of time [e.g., two years], I will be one of those rare artists who makes money. I wonder if you can bear with me during this time and maybe even be on my side? I am presenting an honorable picture of how an artist ought to operate if she wants to make money, and I think you can see that. Yes?

This of course requires that you actually intend to be the exception, take the actions you have outlined, and ultimately make a living. You need to think through your intentions. If you intend to make money as an artist, the above is a good response; if you don't, another sort of response is needed.

How might you meet a family member's charges that you aren't bringing in money from your art when in fact you don't care about the money or suspect that you will never be able to earn much money from your art? Here are a few possible responses:

- To someone (like a parent) not directly affected by how much money you make from your art: "My art is important, meaningful work, and I'm making enough money from my other efforts to live. I don't need much, and I'm living exactly as I want to live. I don't need my art to make me money any more than a monk needs his prayers to make him money. Can you accept my point of view?"
- To a family member (like a breadwinning mate) directly affected by how much money you make from your art: "I do want to contribute, and I know that it's fair to contribute. But can I contribute in ways other

than monetary ways? Can I contribute by being a good friend to you, by loving you, by being available, by doing things that need to get done? Is there a chance we can make that work?"

These are two reasonable approaches. What are some others? Think this through for yourself. Create your talking points to deal with family situations of this sort, and then use them.

CEREMONY: Thinking Thoughts That Serve You

If you grew up in a demanding, critical, or argumentative family or are living in one now, your self-talk is almost guaranteed to turn harsh, punitive, and self-critical. Ceremonially reminding yourself that you want to think only thoughts that serve you can really help with this unfortunate reality. This is different from some related ideas from cognitive therapy that you may already know. Here the focus isn't on whether a thought is rational or irrational, positive or negative, true or false. The focus is on whether or not the thought serves you. If it doesn't serve you, there is no reason to think it!

Thoughts are made up of words, but they arise because of underlying intentions. A thought may arise in order to help you, because you are on your own side and motivated to live proudly and well. Or it may arise because you are feeling sad, angry, defeated, self-critical, or frightened. The words may be exactly the same in either case, but what they mean and what they are doing to you are different. In the first case they are helping you, and in the second they are harming you.

A thought is not serving you if its underlying intention is to defeat you, mock you, or criticize you. Many true, rational thoughts are really self-defeating declarations like "Be scared now!," "Don't try that!," and "You don't have a chance in hell!" A thought like "Wow, there are a lot of people trying to become what I want to become" can mean different things. If for you it means "I had better be savvy, energetic, and fearless," that's fine. However, if it means "I have absolutely no chance," it is not a thought that serves you.

Don't allow yourself to countenance a thought just because a given string of words sounds plausible or truthful. Discern *why* you are stringing those words together. If you've created a thought so as to harm yourself, do not countenance that thought. Instead, have a serious chat with yourself about what's going on underneath. Today, if and when you think a thought that feels "off," don't ask, "Is that a true thought?" or "Is that a rational thought?" Instead, ask yourself, in a calm, serious, ceremonial way, "Where did that thought come from?" and "Is that a thought that serves me?" See if you can begin to discern the origins of the thoughts that harm you. Our thoughts arise for reasons, including self-defeating and self-sabotaging ones. Starting today, begin only to think thoughts that serve you.

Food for Thought

1. To what extent was your family of origin a demanding, critical, or argumentative family?

2. If your family of origin was a demanding, critical, or argumentative family, what were the consequences for you?

3. To what extent is your current family a demanding, critical, or argumentative family?

4. If you currently inhabit a demanding, critical, or argumentative family, how can you make use of your tool kit to deal more effectively with the challenges you're facing?

CHAPTER FOURTEEN

Compulsive and Addicted Families

Growing up in an alcoholic or a drug-addicted family can be highly toxic. Other compulsions and addictions — like addictions to shopping, sex, pornography, or the internet — may seem more benign and are sometimes even socially sanctioned (workaholism, for example). But these compulsions and addictions still have real power to ruin families and, at a minimum, stress out family members and produce adverse psychological consequences.

Take workaholism, for example. Workaholism is different from working hard or working a lot. Working compulsively has less to do with fulfilling your responsibilities or getting the job done than with assuaging some unexpressed fear or meeting some unmet need. You might fear that if you don't work you will face some horrible existential vacuum: you work all the time to avoid feelings of meaninglessness. Or the problem may connect to your home life or unmet relationship needs. Whatever the psychological or existential reasons for workaholism, a person in its grip produces negative psychological consequences at home.

According to the researcher Bryan Robinson:

> Despite the fact that workaholism has been cited as the best-dressed family problem of the twentieth century, the subject has been downplayed or ignored in the family literature, presumably because of cultural maxims that extol its positive aspects while failing to profile the negative aspects of high-performance and workaholism on the family system. Spouses and children of workaholics reported feeling lonely, unloved, isolated, and emotionally and physically abandoned. The clinical literature suggests that many children of workaholics carry the same legacy as their workaholic parents: they become other-directed and approval seeking to meet adult expectations. Recent studies indicated that adult children of workaholics, compared to adult children of non-workaholics, suffer greater depression, higher anxiety, and greater obsessive-compulsive tendencies.

If you're trying to manage and survive in a compulsive or addicted family, you are obliged to recognize that you can't control the situation. Wanting to control leads to an attachment to outcomes and to pain when, as is likely to happen, you discover all over again that you can't have the outcome you hope for. Your dad is still drinking heavily, your sister is still shooting up, or your mother is still eating compulsively. However, you can ask: "Do I want to try to be of some influence in this situation?" Trying to be a little influential doesn't have to lead to an attachment to outcomes. It can help you to be more philosophical and more detached while still hoping to make a difference.

What might it look like to try to exert a little influence? It might look like inviting your sister to come with you to a Narcotics Anonymous meeting: not pressing her, not begging her, but just inviting her in as easy, friendly, and loving a way as you can manage. Will she want to come with you? Almost certainly not, if she is not ready. But if she happens to be ready, your offer might prove lifesaving. You can't control her, but you may — just may — be able to exert some positive influence in her life. You are not obliged to try, but this invitation is a way to offer help without risking too much of your human capital or making yourself too vulnerable.

Carmen's Hungry Family

My client Carmen knew that she and every other member of her family were obese. Yet no one in the family could talk about it. It was the oddest of secrets: they couldn't avoid the evidence of their eyes, yet no mention of the obvious was allowed to escape their lips. Indeed, the family made all sorts of jokes about skinny people, felt entitled to their obesity, got in the face of anyone who suggested that the condition might pose a genuine health problem, and somehow managed to bully the world with their bigness.

Carmen wanted to help her family. I suggested that she start by helping herself. She began following a program based on the principles in my books *Life Purpose Boot Camp* and *The Life Purpose Diet*, and a program called *Diet Like You Mean It!* Its central premise is that effective dieting is essentially about elevating your intention to lose weight to the "high bar" level of life purpose. Slowly but surely, she began to see the positive effects.

But every ounce she lost came at the cost of family strife. Her attempt to lose weight was angering everyone in the family!

Her younger sister's reaction, however, seemed, if not positive, at least neutral. Carmen wondered if she should invite her sister to join her in following the program. We agreed that trying to have an influence on her sister was worth a try, just as long as Carmen didn't get too invested in whether her sister agreed, and as long as Carmen's own efforts wouldn't be threatened if her sister rebuffed her. Carmen created a careful plan for approaching her sister, which included chatting with her away from home and preparing what she wanted to say. As it turned out, her sister enthusiastically agreed to join Carmen in her efforts. As a result, Carmen created an ally in the family — a secret ally at first, but as her sister began to shed pounds and her accomplishments were clear to see, an open and proud ally.

Addiction and Abandonment Issues

A parent with an addiction to alcohol or other problem behavior may abandon you emotionally or literally, leaving you with a lifetime fear of abandonment and extra difficulties in dealing with everyone in your life. How can you speak frankly or bravely to your mate or your children if you fear abandonment? How can you reach out and help someone close to you if you're frightened that your observations may be taken as criticism and provoke your loved one to never speak to you again? The scars left by an alcoholic parent can become open wounds. Here's how Louise, a client of mine, described her abandonment fears:

> I want to help my daughter Bonnie. I want to help her because her husband left her and their three preschool

children in September, and she is trying to deal with her loss. I know I will have trouble helping her because of my tendency to be fearful about her future and about her ability to handle her situation on her own, and because she lashes out at me when she thinks I don't respond appropriately. How can I help her reduce her emotional distress and help her not spiral down into guilt and despair? How can I help her live with her pressing challenges of looking after her young children, living on an unstable income, dealing with her loss, negotiating divorce, and retaining a sense of hope for her future?

I see that it will be a real challenge for me to deal with my own fears and emotions about this situation, including my concern for my young grandchildren and my daughter as well as my own anger towards her husband. At their height, those emotions trigger memories I have from my childhood when my father more or less abandoned our family by descending into alcoholism and unemployment. These memories of abandonment prevent me from being emotionally separate from the current emotions. As I am drawn into her despair, my responses to her become less and less helpful.

What should I do? What can I do? My game plan is to assume that my daughter will come to me when she needs my help. If she doesn't call me, I will assume she is either coping with her situation and emotions or has asked for or is getting support from her sister or one of her friends. My plan also includes helping her to handle her situation in a mature way, for her own sake and self-worth. This means not giving her the impression that I am hovering. But above all else, I must deal with the

way the past — my alcoholic father, fear of abandonment, and all of that — plays itself out right here and
now in the present in my relationship with my daughter.
Her situation raises my demons — and I must deal with
them.

Being Clear and Being Resilient

If you are currently trying to cope within a compulsive or addicted family, or if you are dealing with the residue of family-
of-origin experiences, the tool you will need to pull out of your
tool kit most often is resilience, as you work to distance yourself from your family's problems and assert your own identity
and strengths.

You will also need the tool of clarity. It is tempting to make
up elaborate stories, excuses, or lies as to why, for example, you
do not want to eat the sort of heavy, calorie-laden, excessive
meals that your mother produces three times a day, which
have helped everyone in the family grow obese. Rather than
beat around the bush, be clear. You might say, "I'm keeping to
a 1,600-calorie-a-day eating regimen, and in order to do that,
I have to prepare my own meals," or, "I'm focusing on lots of
vegetables and no desserts, so I'm happy to join you for meals,
but I'm only going to eat what's on my regimen." In the face of
the complaints, criticism, ridicule, and pushback that you may
encounter, you must stay strong, stay brave, and above all stay
clear: "I'm intending to eat according to my regimen. It's my
choice."

And what if your mother responds with "Well, go buy
your own food with your own money, you ungrateful, hurtful, spiteful, miserable daughter!"? Continue to be clear: "All
right, I will." Do not let yourself be emotionally blackmailed

into compulsive or addictive behaviors. Fight for your right to be healthy, even if it makes you enemies with your family, and even if it makes your family life more difficult rather than easier.

Creatives in Recovery

As a family therapist and a coach who has worked with creative and performing artists for more than thirty years, I know that creative people can experience special compulsion and addiction issues. On top of the common challenges that any person experiences in early recovery — including the cravings, the longings, the triggers, the old habits, and the peer pressure to use — additional important challenges face the creative person. The primary challenge is that creating itself can prove a threat to recovery.

Say that you're a creative person and you realize that your addiction has gotten the better of you. You bravely decide to enter into recovery. The main stance of early recovery is to not get your system "wild" or "worked up" or your mind "driven." You are trying to calmly pay attention to the tasks of recovery by living "one day at a time" and by taking care of "first things first." But creating inherently involves seeking to be wild and driven. How do you reconcile your recovery with your creative needs and energies?

The very act of creating is a voyage into the unknown (a voyage that provokes anxiety), a command to send your brain racing (so that it can obsess productively), and an exploration of your deepest thoughts and feelings (with all the dangers associated with traveling to those depths). Recovery requires calmness and creating requires wildness: and therefore the wildness of creating can endanger recovery.

Given this reality, you will want to adopt the following five tactics for creating in early recovery.

- *Put recovery first.* As much as you may want to get back to creating, your recovery comes first. If you have a choice between attending an AA meeting or painting for another hour, going to the meeting is the wise choice. If you have a choice between starting the day with a mindfulness meditation that supports your recovery or starting right in on your sculpting, the mindfulness meditation comes first. This isn't what your creative nature wants: it wants to create. But in early recovery your mantra should be "Recovery comes first."

- *Choose projects wisely.* Early recovery is not the time to overwhelm yourself or to add high anxiety to your life. If, for example, you have the choice between executing one painting that is less taxing and another that is more taxing, your creative nature may want to tackle the more ambitious project. But if you keep your recovery needs in clear focus, it is wise to opt for the less taxing project. This may feel disappointing, but you can remind yourself that you have the opportunity to create a powerful body of work over time — but only if you maintain your sobriety and your recovery. That may help put the choice in perspective.

- *Monitor your energy, your mind, and your mood as you create.* As you're engaged in creating, you have the job of avoiding getting too wound up or thinking thoughts that jeopardize your recovery (like "This painting is so bad, I'm going to need a good stiff drink when I'm done with it!"), and not propelling yourself into a dangerous mood, whether a manic mood or a despairing one. As you create, you will want to keep one eye on the tasks of recovery: if you are getting too bleak, too manic, or too self-critical, you must warn yourself, "Careful! I'm threatening my recovery here!" Then you must immediately do whatever you know to do when your recovery is threatened, such as calling your sponsor, attending a twelve-step meeting, or listening to a recovery tape.

- *Leave creative stints mindfully.* Creating starts us racing. We get wound up, wired, excited, and agitated as we bite into our current project. Many creative folks crave alcohol, drugs, or sex after creating because they need to "come down and calm down." In this very real sense, creating is a trigger and puts you in harm's way. You will want to prepare a smart ritual or ceremony to employ when you leave your creating that reminds you powerfully that your job is to return to the rest of the day calmly. You want to announce to yourself that you are leaving all of that energy, excitement, and agitation safely behind you.

- *Monitor your choices.* In early recovery, you need to be alert to threats to your recovery. You make the time to ask yourself questions like "Is my current creative project the appropriate one, given my recovery needs?" or "Is there anything about the way I'm living my creative life that's a threat to my recovery?" If your answer to the first question is no, you make a change and work on a safer, wiser project. If your answer to the second question is yes, you face that challenge squarely and do whatever is necessary. That might mean giving up an old drinking buddy or avoiding an old haunt.

Creating is a life-purpose choice and a meaning opportunity. But everything falls apart if recovery fails. Use these five tactics and your tool kit to ensure that your desire to create doesn't threaten your recovery.

CEREMONY: Not Tripping Repeatedly in the Very Same Spot

One of the hallmarks of the addictive and compulsive personality is repeating a behavior and unreasonably expecting a different outcome. If you've grown up in a family marred by addiction and compulsion or are currently trying to survive in such a family, you, too, may fall into this mindset and get into the terrible habit of repeating behaviors that you know don't serve you.

Imagine that you are doing a beautiful job of maintaining your mental health and your emotional wellbeing, and suddenly you're challenged by a trip to the dentist, a visit from your mother, a broken promise by your mate, or an extra work assignment. Here it comes — that place where you regularly trip and fall into old emotional patterns. You can see it coming, but is the danger really registering?

- You know that the visit to the dentist will not only trigger panic but will completely change your personality, from the person you've been working to become to that other person who lived out of control for all of her twenties and thirties. Can you see that danger coming?

- You know that the impending visit from your mother will create an extraordinary amount of lethargy and sadness in you, make you hypercritical, and leave you with a bad taste in your mouth for weeks after she's left. Can you see that danger coming?
- You know that another broken promise by your mate will create all sorts of sour feelings in you and between the two of you, including revenge fantasies, doubts about the viability of the relationship, thoughts about leaving, and a bout of severe sadness. Can you see that danger coming?
- You know that your job is already only barely tolerable, and if your boss springs some extra work on you on Friday afternoon, forcing you to catch the late train home, that will ruin your weekend: you'll yell at your mate and your children and be tempted to kick the dog. Can you see that danger coming?

If you know from past experience that an event of this sort will trip you up, you can use the warning to try to prevent that reaction, including readying the right tools from your tool kit. Choose any tool you have that helps you not trip repeatedly over the very same crack in the pavement.

In recovery work, this impending event is called a trigger. For someone who trips and falls around alcohol, the trigger might be the annual holiday party at work, a visit from an old drinking buddy, or a business situation that puts you among heavy drinkers. In recovery programs you're taught to identify these triggers, take them seriously, and know clearly what you will do when you face them.

For someone in recovery, the response might be to call your sponsor or attend a twelve-step meeting. Or it might be to skip the holiday party, to arrange to see your old buddy in the safety of your own home, or to let your coworkers know that you are in recovery and can't hang out with them. Because you are taking the danger seriously, you might need to do one, several, or all of these things.

To recognize your own triggers and create a menu of things to do when faced with them is real work that you may want to do. For now, though, you can do just one simple, easy ceremonial thing: practice saying, adamantly and clearly, "I'm not tripping there." Picture one of your triggers — that visit from your mother, that broken promise by your mate — picture it without flinching, say, "I'm not tripping there," and explain to yourself what you will do to handle that specific challenge when it confronts you.

Our road through life is uneven. The road is cracked and buckled, creating innumerable chances for us to trip and fall. We come to know some of these cracks only by tripping over them and falling headfirst. But many others are visible to us from a distance, and we can prepare ourselves so that we don't trip and fall. Maybe we will still stumble a little, or maybe we won't stumble at all.

Wouldn't avoiding the fall prove a welcome relief and spare you emotional scrapes and bruises?

As much work as we may do to keep ourselves mentally healthy, triggers can still make us lose our balance. When you see one of these triggers coming, take it seriously. Exclaim, "I'm not tripping there!" and mean it.

Food for Thought

1. To what extent was your family of origin a compulsive or addicted family?
2. If your family of origin was a compulsive or addicted family, what were the consequences for you?
3. To what extent is your current family a compulsive or addicted family?
4. If you currently inhabit a compulsive or addicted family, how can you use your tool kit to deal more effectively with the challenges you're facing?

CHAPTER FIFTEEN

Rule-Bound, Intrusive, and Authoritarian Families

Many families are ruled by iron hands. In these families, you follow the rules or else you are punished. You are carefully observed and monitored, your movements are restricted, your ideas are constrained, and the flavor of the family is authoritarian. The rules may be religious or cultural rules or the idiosyncratic rules of the family's authoritarian leader. In each case the ruler's intention is the same: to run the family like a cult.

Toxic family-of-origin rules tend to produce a lifetime of relationship problems for children who grow up in them. According to the authors of one study, "Dysfunctional rules hinder communication, weaken relationships, and produce rebellion, resistance, chaos, fear, and low self-esteem in the family and its members. Researchers have found positive relationships between perceived dysfunctional family of origin rules and internalized shame in adult offspring, problems establishing intimacy in young adult intimate relationships, and dating anxiety, relationship dissatisfaction, and problems with commitment in young adult intimate relationships."

Any family has its rules: for example, "We are orthodox Jews, and we keep kosher." In addition, individual family members in the family have their own rules: for example, "I am always right, and I must dominate and win every conversation and interaction." Family members may operate by the same or different personal rules. If everyone in a family holds to the rule that he or she is always right, it should be clear what family life will look and feel like!

Barbara, a client of mine, told me:

My sister is completely stubborn about everything. But so am I. My gut reaction is that when I am stubborn about something, my ego is all wrapped up in it. I try to stop myself in my mental tracks. I ask myself, Is this a belief or habit that was once useful and no longer serving me to my highest good? Usually the answer is no; if that were the case, it would be·a bit easier to see this and to discontinue my old thought patterns. The next question to ask is: Am I holding on to this belief or habit because I need to be "right" and therefore by doing so, make someone else "wrong"?

I think that's usually the case. Everyone in our family needs to be right all of the time, no matter what! Next question: Who or what needs to be "wrong" for my ego to feel good about itself? My ego is not often found to have my heart and soul's best interest in mind. I would attempt to walk through this thought process with myself — and maybe with my sister, too, if she would let me. I am getting up the courage to try this — first with myself. It's going to be really hard, I think, because everyone in my family genuinely hates being wrong!

Another common personal rule is "I will never listen to anybody." Such rules are often applied or ignored in complicated and contradictory ways. My client John described his relationship with his brother:

I know that my brother is stubborn, but I also know that, in spite of his stubbornness, he takes my words very seriously, which is one of the reasons that he becomes very defensive when I talk to him. He doesn't want to accept anything that other people say to him at face value without digesting it and arriving at his own conclusions, except when some idea seems to be a shortcut to something he wants.

In the past, when I told him things in a neutral and nonthreatening way, even if his first response was to defend an alternative to my suggestion, he would think about it in his own time and sometimes come around to realize some value in my suggestion and apply it in some way. That has become my technique for handing off advice to him. However, at this time, he is very bent on making a dramatic change in his life and is being prompted by some people who have their own motivations. He is not being at all receptive to any suggestions that don't align with his immediate goals.

I feel that I have to say my piece tactfully, and then it's up to him to evaluate it for himself. I wish there was a more direct way to convey advice so that he would be more receptive, but it seems there are always intermediate steps where he initially rejects, then considers, then comes to some understanding. This is such a slow process, especially in the middle of a crisis! But he is who he is, his stubbornness is real, and I don't know of any other way that has the slightest chance of getting through to him.

Being Brave and Strong When Family Rules Aren't Right

Family rules vary widely, from the benign to the seriously cruel. Many families are awash in rigid rules: Sit at the dinner table until you've finished everything on your plate! Sit up straight while you're at it! And no talking! Take out exactly three toys to play with. If there's a fourth you might want to play with, too bad! Do your chores perfectly or get punished! And so on.

There's nothing wrong with rules per se. You can't do math without mathematical rules. Traffic can't move properly without the rules of the road. But how much mental and emotional well-being can possibly flow from the following sorts of rules?

- You must not shut the door when you go to the bathroom.
- You must pray a certain number of times each day.
- You must not speak unless you've been spoken to.
- You must not date someone outside your race, religion, or group.
- You must not adopt "the homosexual lifestyle."
- You must not go to college, because you're a girl.

If your family has a rule about taking off your shoes when you enter the house, that rule most likely doesn't make you feel overcontrolled, diminished, or violated. But what about not shutting the door when you go to the bathroom? How does that make you feel? And how can its intention be anything but sinister? How could such a rule come from anywhere but a cruel, unhealthy place? Isn't the intent to ridicule and humiliate? Some family rules are clearly just wrong!

Thoughtful parents don't want to be too intrusive, restrictive, or rule-bound, but they want to be aware of what is actually going on with their children. My client Sandra was concerned that her teenage son might have a drinking problem. She really wanted to know what he was up to, but she didn't want to intrude too much on his privacy or become too vigilant about his movements. We tried to define what seemed like reasonable and necessary oversight and vigilance and what felt too intrusive.

She decided that she needed to know whether her son was hiding alcohol around the house, whether she could smell alcohol on his skin (a surer sign of alcohol abuse than smelling alcohol on the breath), and whether he was home when he claimed on the phone to be home. On the other hand, she decided that she would not follow him when he left the house, that she would not try to read his emails or text messages, and that she would not question his friends or their parents about his behavior. She had no idea if this was the perfect line to walk, but it felt like a reasonable one.

Family Authoritarianism

Parents in strict, rule-bound families are functionally tyrants. This tyranny produces all sorts of consequences in their children. According to the website Positive Parenting Ally:

> Research has shown that children of authoritarian families are more prone to suffering from low self-esteem and low self-worth than children coming from authoritative or permissive parents. In this way the short-term behavioral gain of obedience is heavily outweighed by the long-term psychological damage. The effect of

punishments is that the child will be well-behaved out of fear and not because he or she feels like it or has understood the true meaning of a positive and caring attitude. In this way the child learns that love and acceptance is dependent on good behavior. The results are low self-esteem and inferiority complexes, a lack of basic trust in people, a passive attitude to their own role in life, adherence to rigid traditions, a fear of experimentation, mental rigidity and oversimplified thinking, self-guilt and shame, the sense that brute force, whether physical or verbal, is the only real power, and poor socializing skills.

Following World War II, there was some excellent work done on authoritarianism. Theodor Adorno, the German-born sociologist, collaborated with Else Frenkel-Brunswik, a psychoanalyst and German émigré, and the social psychologists Daniel Levinson and Nevitt Sanford at the University of California, Berkeley, to investigate the "authoritarian personality." They took as their starting point the Freudian model of the psyche and argued that a certain sort of punitive, rigid, and conventional upbringing produced a child, and then an adult, forced to control his or her roiling id with a punitive and rigid superego.

They believed that certain traits naturally arose from this particular dynamism. They concluded that the authoritarian personality comprised nine qualities or psychological orientations, among them aggressiveness, cynical destructiveness, anti-intellectualism, a superstitious nature, exaggerated concerns about sex, and, in the followers of authoritarian leaders, what they called "authoritarian submission." They concerned themselves more with trying to understand the motives and psychology of the followers than of the leaders themselves, arguing that a tyrannical would-be leader was a relatively innocuous proposition if he or she didn't then attract millions of followers.

Bob Altemeyer, a leading contemporary writer on authoritarianism and the authoritarian personality, observes in *The Authoritarians:* "Authoritarianism is something authoritarian followers and authoritarian leaders cook up between themselves. It happens when the followers submit too much to the leaders, trust them too much, and give them too much leeway to do whatever they want — which often is something undemocratic, tyrannical and brutal.... [T]he greatest threat to American democracy today arises from a militant authoritarianism that has become a cancer upon the nation." He goes on to ask why authoritarian followers act the way they do. "Why do their leaders so often turn out to be crooks and hypocrites? Why are both the followers and the leaders so aggressive that hostility is practically their trademark?...In a democracy, a wannabe tyrant is just a comical figure on a soapbox unless a huge wave of supporters lifts him to high office.... [In Nazi Germany,] ultimately the problem lay in the followers."

This pattern is reflected within families, too. Dad may be the authoritarian; but it is the way that other family members follow along and adopt his prejudices and cruelties that make it so hard on any family member who wants to stand up to him. You're not standing up just to Dad: you have a whole army to battle. That is heavy lifting for one person!

Tiger Moms (and Dads) and Negative Outcomes

Strict, rule-bound, restrictive, and intrusive families are not necessarily cruel families. In some instances the strictness is

applied for the sake of what are perceived to be beneficial outcomes, like children's future social and financial success. But
even if no cruelty is intended, the felt experience in such a family situation is often one of harshness and cruelty, and it can result in outcomes like sadness, anxiety, low self-esteem (despite
all that a child may accomplish), and a basic inability to relate.

A CBS news report featured a study at the University of
California, Berkeley, that followed more than 250 Chinese American immigrant families with first- and second-grade children in
the San Francisco Bay Area for over two years. "We found that
children whose parents use more authoritarian-type parenting
strategies tend to develop more aggression, depression, anxiety,
and social problems and have poorer social skills," said Qing
Zhou, an assistant professor of psychology who led the research.
The report continued: "Kim Wong Keltner, a Chinese American
writer from San Francisco, said…that many Asian American
kids are so compelled to excel at academics and keep a low profile that they don't feel comfortable, let alone permitted, to ex-
plore their creative sides.…As a result, she said their social skills
are lagging by the time they get out in the real world."

If this has been your experience, you will want to bravely
engage in some self-examination and discern how the pressures placed on you to excel and succeed have influenced your
formed personality. If you can make those connections, using
your skills of clarity, presence, and awareness, you may find
the way to lift a lifetime of sadness, panic attacks, or low self-
esteem. If you were pushed unnaturally and criticized overtly
or silently, you were left operating by rules that you may not
be aware of and that may not be serving you at all. It is time
to examine those rules. You have enough freedom and enough
available personality to do so, if you can muster your strength
and courage!

CEREMONY: My Mantra

If you are, or have been, watched, pressured, punished, and otherwise subjected to the stress of a rule-bound, intrusive, or authoritarian family, one small but useful exercise that you can engage in is creating a mantra. A mantra is a ceremonial phrase that you silently intone and repeat — in this case, one that reminds you that you have internal resources, that you have not given up on life, and that you know your life purposes; or a mantra that does some other important work in helping you feel safe and strong.

Here are three examples of mantras that clients of mine created and their reasons for creating them:

- *Jennifer:* "I decided on 'The Breath of Life' as my mantra. I chose it because it reminds me to breathe deeply when there's tension or anxiety and to breathe deeply simply for health and vitality. When my focus starts with my breath, it centers and grounds me, and I feel more inner directed, rather than scattered with tasks or activities. And it also allows me the space to stay in tune with the bigger perspective of my life."
- *Leslie:* "For my mantra I chose 'Embrace the integrity of what is.' I chose that short phrase because it encompasses what I see myself doing as a woman and as an artist. It puts me squarely in the truth of the moment and reflects what I believe is so important, to actively accept what is in all its integrity. It reminds me that it is not my will that creates

the moment but a much larger design for life of which I am a small but vital part."

- *Amanda:* "I chose 'I am the light of my own life.' I think light has many qualities that I want to bring into my life. It is creative, transformative, and healing. From a metaphorical perspective, I have clearer vision and fresh insight when I see the light. I need a certain light to work in and to be productive, and the right light also positively affects my mood and emotions. My mantra helps me to think that I carry that light within me rather than needing to find optimal light from a source other than myself."

Create your own mantra and ceremonially use it throughout the day; and in that small way and in other small and large ways, including making good use of your tool kit, courageously deal with the heavy consequences of living in a rule-bound, intrusive, or authoritarian family.

Food for Thought

1. To what extent was your family of origin a rule-bound, intrusive, or authoritarian family?
2. If your family of origin was rule-bound, intrusive, or authoritarian, what were the consequences for you?
3. To what extent is your current family rule-bound, intrusive, or authoritarian?
4. If you currently inhabit a rule-bound, intrusive, or authoritarian family, how can you make use of your tool kit to deal more effectively with the challenges you're facing?

CHAPTER SIXTEEN

Dramatic and Chaotic Families

Some families seem defined by dramas and chaos. The dramas may involve slammed doors, operatic gestures, noisy fights, minor and major accidents, sudden outsized gestures — Mom rushing off to become a cloistered nun, returning home three months later with a new boyfriend — and much more. The chaos may take the form of household disorganization, missed appointments, mislaid documents, chronic tardiness, and crises ranging from letting the dog run away to inexplicable medical emergencies.

An outsider is likely to shake his head at the chaos and disorganization, wondering, "How can anybody live like that?" Inside the family, no one is immune to the chaos and drama, even when they are shaking their heads and wondering what in heaven's name is going on. The whole family appears trapped in the storm, including those who are searching for the eye of the hurricane and desperately wishing that calmness might prevail. But a day or a week without a crisis or a drama is inevitably followed by some new whirlwind.

Family therapists who work in the tradition of Virginia Satir, one of the founders of modern family therapy, emphasize the idea that you can eliminate something unwanted (like chaos) in a family system only if genuine transformational change occurs in the system. Any superficial remedy is, like a Band-Aid, bound to come off over time. Carl Sayles describes this process of genuine transformation:

> The goal is to change and transform the behavior, not to eliminate it. When we attempt to eradicate something in our lives, the physical and emotional cost is often very high, frequently resulting in people returning to a prior level of coping. Looking at change through this transformational lens, we can help people in the process of discovery, awareness building, and understanding, transforming their survival stances into more congruent ways of speaking their truth at that moment in time. Feelings that previously controlled a person are felt and acknowledged, putting the person in charge of these feelings that once controlled them. Transformation happens as people take charge of their feelings, perceptions, expectations, and yearnings.

How is family transformation of this sort accomplished? A family therapist might say it can't be done without outside expert help. Indeed, there is hardly anything more powerfully transforming than a family's spending time with a genuinely masterful family therapist who can settle them down, deal with the chaos and disorganization that they bring right into the consulting room (like the dust cloud that the *Peanuts* character Pig-Pen travels with), and quietly and calmly help the family members see what is going on and help them identify and announce changes that they are willing to undertake.

Working with individual clients is a cakewalk compared to working with families! I spent many years working with artist couples and artists' families as a therapist before making the transition to creativity coaching. One of the ways I started working with a family was by asking each family member if he or she was keeping a secret from the rest of the family. I didn't ask them to *share* the secret; I only asked if they had one. One by one, each family member admitted harboring a secret that it felt unsafe to share. This opening gambit set the tone for sessions: family members understood that we were going to talk about real things but that I wasn't going to press them to say or do things that would make them feel unsafe.

Chaos Then and Chaos Now

Most chaotic families are not blessed with the sort of transformation that family therapy can offer, and as a result, family members carry the legacy of chaos and disorganization with them into adulthood. Beverly, a coaching client, described her experience this way:

> I was raised in a chaotic environment, one of seven children, by two social drinkers, Art and Jo. My parents had three boys and then four girls. I am the fifth child. That home was completely chaotic, and my present home is likewise chaotic. I have been living with a man I adore and who has been driving me up the wall for seventeen years — a first in terms of how long I've ever been with anybody. All my other relationships only lasted two or three years.

Well, our home is a mess. I have the dining-room table strewn with mail, papers, knickknacks, and books. There are shopping bags and boxes filled with stuff all around it.

The kitchen is somewhat organized — it's beautiful, really. Charlie decorated it. The bathroom is clean. Charlie and I spent a weekend day organizing and tossing out our stuff. Then we did a deep cleaning. We've kept it clean for at least this past month. Our bedroom is a mess, with my clothes strewn all over the place, piles of clothes collecting on the floor, unread books piling up by the bed. There's opened but unread mail on the nightstand. My life has always been this tension between chaos and organization, with chaos winning much of the time. I started out with too much chaos and, as hard as I try and with the successes I do sometimes achieve, I still end up with too much chaos.

Laura's Avoidance of Drama

One result of growing up in a dramatic and chaotic family is that you can develop a powerful, anxiety-driven need to avoid drama and chaos at all costs. This can turn a person into a timid, weaker version of herself, into someone who is always vigilant, deeply risk-averse, and supercontrolled. To take one example of an unfortunate result of this sort, consider a coaching client of mine by the name of Laura.

Laura had grown up in a family of actors who at times achieved significant success. Her mother played important character roles in major motion pictures and won accolades for her performances. For several years her father had a major supporting role in a long-running television drama. At other times, and for long stretches, one or both of them were out of work. Whether working or not, they managed to sustain a fantastically high level of chaos and drama.

Her mother once came at her father with a knife. Her father brought his mistress to a family party. Her mother had attempted suicide more than once. Her father had been bailed out of countless drunken situations that, if he'd been less of a celebrity, would have landed him in jail. Their friends, too, were dramatic in all the ways one might expect: drug overdoses, destroyed hotel rooms, trips to the emergency room, scandals, and cover-ups.

As a result, Laura had grown into a prim woman who maintained a high level of vigilance and control, felt uneasy altering her routines in any way, and compulsively and anxiously sought order in her life. She worked in a bank, where she was a model employee and maintained cordial relationships with everyone but felt close to no one. Nor did she have friends or an intimate other. She came to me with the complaint that I hear a lot: her life didn't feel meaningful to her. She felt shut down, closed off, and at a loss.

She described her childhood. I asked her if that family chaos had caused her to shut down. Tearfully, she agreed that it had. Somehow it had come with the cost of taking the fun out of life. Even thinking of taking a risk — a risk as small as wearing a bright color — made her sick to her stomach. I invited her to learn about the eight-skills tool kit, and a few weeks later I asked her which tool she thought might help the most right now in aiding her to escape from her cocoon.

She thought about that and replied, "Strength and courage seem like the obvious ones. But I think there's something that has to come before those two. I think it's actually clarity. I think

I have to say some clear things to myself about what happened in the past and about what I want for myself now. Maybe being able to say those clear things actually requires strength and courage, so I guess I need all three — clarity, strength, and courage."

I asked her what concretely she wanted to attempt. For a long moment nothing came to her. Then she said, "I need to take one small risk." Asked if she could identify one, she replied immediately, "Wearing bright colors at work." It may seem odd that changing her outfit might be the first step on the road to recovering from growing up in a dramatic, chaotic family, but Laura was clear that it was exactly the right first step. "And it won't be easy," she said, smiling a little. "It may sound like nothing to you, but to me it's a big deal — a scary big deal. I hope I can do it!" As it turned out, she couldn't do it the next Monday or Tuesday. But on Wednesday, she did. The return journey had begun.

Being Aware in a Dramatic and Chaotic Family

The noise and energy of a chaotic and dramatic family can make your head spin and cause you to live a reactive life rather than a reflective life. How can you maintain awareness in the middle of all of this?

First, you can create and maintain an awareness or mindfulness practice. Done consistently and turned into a real habit, this kind of practice is strong enough to withstand family hurricanes. It might be as simple as journaling every morning or evening, or as elaborate as a lengthy sitting meditation in the company of others at a Buddhist center or a wellness center.

Without some practice of this sort in place, one that you turn to every day without fail, it's all too easy for the drama and chaos of your family life to overwhelm you. Start your practice today!

Here are five tips for dealing with drama and chaos:

- *Don't jump in.* Drama is like a pool that invites you to plunge in. It glistens; it beckons. If your day has been boring, a family drama might look like an attractive alternative to the boredom. Maybe you're stressed out, and jumping into the family drama would give you a way to relieve stress by yelling, accusing, and wringing your hands. Stop. Don't jump in cavalierly or unnecessarily.

- *Change the language.* Everyone is bewailing the fact that the Thanksgiving turkey got overcooked. "Thanksgiving's ruined!" "God, we'll have to order pizza!" "Mom, I was looking forward to this meal all year!" Don't go along with all this dramatic handwringing. Instead, internally change and normalize your language. "Have a lot of cranberry sauce and enjoy yourself!" "The dark meat is still moist, and I love the dark meat!" Resolve privately not to call things tragedies when they amount to little more than disappointments or inconveniences.

- *Create mantras of peace and quiet.* When dramas are percolating and exploding all around you, say, "All is peace and light," "Deep inner quiet," or some other mantra that calms you, quiets your inner turbulence, and shields you from the surrounding storm. You might think your mantra, you might say it under your breath, or you might say it out loud — but quietly.

- *Leave the scene.* Make your local library your bastion of quiet, safety, and sanity. Go to the cafeteria at your local junior college, buy a taco, and let the stress drain out of you. Let the soothing energy of a busy coffeehouse replace the upsetting chaos of your family life. Go to the movies and vicariously travel to a faraway place and time where, in the drawing room of some country manor, characters are conversing without yelling. Get out of the house — try not to feel or act trapped there!

- *Visualize a ceremony in which you are crowned the king or queen of "no drama."* In this unique court, the absence of drama is honored! The court motto is "No intrigues, please!" Incipient dramas are nipped in the bud with grace and wit. This is your kingdom. Picture your loyal subjects revering you because of the amazing talent you have for exemplifying calmness and a complete lack of histrionics.

CEREMONY: Tolerating a Difficult Thought for Ten Seconds

When we get frustrated, we don't like the feeling, and so we do something to quickly relieve it: maybe something safe and innocent like watching a movie, maybe something more dangerous and reckless like binge drinking or driving at twice the speed limit. We need to learn to tolerate frustrations better than this so that we can actually deal with what's frustrating us. The following ceremony can help.

Maybe there's some big, difficult thing that you know that you need to do: changing your job, separating from your mate, or stopping your drinking. Maybe it's a smaller change than that but one that still feels like a gigantic challenge. Maybe it's admitting that you are unhappy with the way your adult son is acting, unhappy with the way you abandon your resolutions at the first hint of difficulty, or unhappy with the way you create unnecessary drama in your life.

Thinking a thought that announces your frustrations, like "My husband really is an alcoholic!" or "I absolutely must leave my wife!" is likely to produce panic. It makes the issue feel so huge, dangerous, and consequential that you can't get anywhere near tackling it, or even thinking about it. You think, "My son is not acting respectfully toward me," bite your lip, dismiss the thought, and continue to let him insult you. Not being able to tolerate one's own thoughts is a key component of denial.

Tolerating a difficult thought is much harder than people realize. Because it's difficult and because we get defensive, it's important to create a ceremony to help support us in our efforts.

Try thinking a thought that agitates you. Let's say it's "I need a divorce." Do you go blank instantly? Do you have physical sensations, like nausea or light-headedness, that are associated with panic? Are you barraged and assaulted by thoughts like "If I leave him, I'll suddenly be poor," "I've never worked a day in my life," "I'll feel like such a failure!," "Children of divorce have so many problems!," "What will I say to my priest?," and "My parents will give me *such* a look when I tell them"? What actually happens when you try to think this particular difficult thought?

Pick a thought that you do not want to think. Set a timer for ten seconds. Think that thought for the full ten seconds. That's all you need to do. Just "be with" the thought for ten seconds. Don't worry about doing anything with the thought or with the feelings that may flood you as you try to stay with that difficult thought. You don't have to dispute them, answer them, handle them, or accept them. You just have to survive them. You just have to tolerate them. Your goal is to learn how to remain in the presence of difficult thoughts for a full ten seconds and not run away.

Doing this simple thing may itself feel horribly hard. But in order to make the changes that we need to make in life, including managing our sadness, anxiety, and addictive tendencies and dealing with the fallout from a dramatic and chaotic family life, a first step is tolerating disturbing thoughts, thoughts that are fraught with consequences. Learning to do this creates calmness and an opening for growth and change. You begin to see that you can survive the feeling of panic that comes with thinking a difficult thought. This makes it possible to contemplate decisions and action steps.

Big change is hard — and trying to think about big change may be even harder. Bringing up difficult thoughts creates whirlwinds and hurricanes. By learning how to bravely weather these storms, you give yourself a better chance of making the changes likely to improve your emotional health. Pick a difficult thought, think it, and then quietly count to ten. That's all. Accomplishing that seemingly simple task may work wonders.

Food for Thought

1. To what extent was your family of origin a dramatic or chaotic family?
2. If your family of origin was a dramatic or chaotic family, what were the consequences for you?
3. To what extent is your current family a dramatic or chaotic family?
4. If you currently inhabit a dramatic or chaotic family, how can you use your tool kit to deal more effectively with the challenges you're facing?

CHAPTER SEVENTEEN

Acquisitive and Materialistic Families

We haven't really examined the problems that arise when your values clash with the dominant values in your family. The clash might be over religious, political, career, or personal values, or, as is so often the case with my creative and performing-artist clients, over whether pursuing a creative career is a reasonable, worthy path or a self-indulgent dead end.

Clashes like this can destroy families. Think of the Civil War, when brothers often took opposite sides and sometimes even killed one another on the battlefield. When your values clash with the dominant values in your family, conflict is inevitable. It may remain repressed and unexpressed, or it may boil over into arguments and estrangements.

Values matter; they possess psychological and emotional importance; and if you feel that someone else's values are misguided or, worse, base and immoral, you are going to have an ongoing problem with that person. One such value clash occurs when a given family member internally or openly objects to the way that other family members are invested in accumulating material possessions, in caring too much about name brands and designer labels, and in being just plain too crass and acquisitive.

This conflict can be conceptualized as the clash between material values and spiritual values, or between material values and existential values. I see it as the clash between a person who would like to live her life according to her life-purpose choices and other family members who, in her view, are using material things as substitutes for authentic living. If this is your experience, you may hold your peace — and then feel compelled to erupt and act out in the following sorts of situations:

- You think a reasonably priced bottle of wine is appropriate to bring to a dinner party that you're attending, but your husband insists on getting an expensive, top-shelf bottle whose cost "could feed three starving children for a week."
- You attend a Christmas party at your sister's house and are appalled by the large number of presents her children are receiving.
- Your nephew's bar mitzvah turns out to be an over-the-top, six-figure extravaganza.
- Your wife insists that the kitchen needs updating and remodeling, even though you remodeled it three years ago.
- Your son throws a tantrum because you won't buy him the hottest new athletic shoes, costing several hundred dollars.
- Your parents, who have refused to let you go on the annual school trip to a theater festival or to rent an oboe for your music class, spend a small fortune on their Hawaiian vacation, gushing to you and your

brother about how "very pricey" it will be — as if spending more rather than less were some sort of accomplishment.

In an article called "The Madness of Materialism," Steve Taylor writes:

Once our basic material needs are satisfied, our level of income makes little difference to our level of happiness. Research has shown, for example, that extremely rich people such as billionaires are not significantly happier than people with an average income, and suffer from higher levels of depression. Researchers in positive psychology have concluded that true well-being does not come from wealth but from other factors such as good relationships, meaningful and challenging jobs or hobbies, and a sense of connection to something bigger than ourselves (such as a religion, a political or social cause, or a sense of mission).

In some families, it is the parents who want things and the children who make faces at their acquisitive nature. Nowadays, with children bombarded with ads and growing ever more brand conscious, it may be the other way around: the children may be the materialist, acquisitive ones, and the parents may be the ones shaking their heads. The authors at Campaign for a Commercial-Free Childhood report:

Children who are more materialistic are less happy, more depressed, more anxious and have lower self-esteem.

Exposure to media and marketing promotes materialistic values in children and is stressful for families.

Conflict between parents and children is directly related to children's exposure to advertising....

- This generation of children is the most brand-conscious ever. Teenagers today have 145 conversations about brands per week.
- 44% of 4th through 8th graders report daydreaming 'a lot' about being rich. Marketers deliberately encourage children to nag their parents for products.
- Nagging accounts for one in three trips to fast food restaurants.

Gaining Clarity about What Promotes Happiness

If you're dealing with a values conflict like this in your family, your main objective is to stay true to your vision of what matters in life and what constitutes ethical action. One way to do this, and avoid succumbing to the bombardment of inducements to buy the newest, best, and shiniest of everything, is to remember that our emotional well-being flows not from possessions but from our efforts to actually live our life purposes. Use your new skills, especially the skills of clarity and awareness, to help you remember this vital lesson.

Things do not make us happy — and even if they could, living for happiness is not our objective. Living with purpose makes a person happier than trying to be happy! To live for an experience — of joy, of meaning, of pleasure, of happiness, of anything — rather than for a purpose is to put your emotional life in danger, since you are living for temporary outcomes that, even if achieved, provide only fleeting satisfaction. Living your life purposes provides a much deeper satisfaction.

Outcomes like "happiness" become more elusive if you are chasing them. How deeply pleasurable is food if you are always chasing food, always craving food, always hungry for the next potato chip or cinnamon roll? When you were nine, how long did the toy you desperately wanted really amuse you once you received it? We want to be happy, but chasing happiness is not the answer. Doing what matters is the answer!

Consider this study by Steven Cole and his team of researchers, as reported by the Mother Nature Network:

> The researchers assessed and took blood samples from 80 healthy adults who were classified as having either hedonic or eudaimonic well-being. Hedonic well-being is defined as happiness gained from seeking pleasure; eudaimonic well-being is that gained by having a deep sense of purpose and meaning in life....The study showed that people who had high levels of eudaimonic well-being showed favorable profiles with low levels of inflammatory gene expression and exhibited a strong expression of antiviral and antibody genes. For the pleasure seekers, the opposite was true; those with high levels of hedonic well-being showed an adverse gene-expression profile, giving high inflammation and low antiviral/antibody expression.

You achieve this happiness that runs deeper than pleasure seeking by living a life oriented around and in alignment with your life purposes. You identify your life purposes; you announce that you stand behind them; you live them; you create meaning as you live them; and you produce a deep happiness, a happiness that produces physical and emotional health. You aren't chasing anything — not a bestseller, an orgasm, another high, another conquest, a million dollars: you are simply doing the next right thing in accordance with your understanding of your values and principles. You are quietly and calmly living, rather than avidly chasing.

To live like this, you must believe that you matter. So many of the clients I work with, despite the optimistic face they put on it, don't really believe that the short story, watercolor, or song that they are struggling so hard to create is really worth the trouble. Does the world really need another short story, watercolor, or song? Why bother? Once you are pestered by the question of whether what you are doing "really" matters, unless the answer is an immediate and unequivocal yes, you will be haunted by that question and experience a meaning crisis.

When this happens, you begin to lose the emotional and physical benefits of living your life purposes because you have begun to doubt them. You've pulled the rug out from under yourself, as it were, and you've opened yourself up to emotional and physical distress. This is why "meaning repair" is such an important part of the process of healing your heart and keeping yourself well. You must quietly affirm that what you are doing does indeed matter; or, if you have come to believe that it really doesn't, then you must choose another path. Until you do one of these two things, your emotional health will be threatened, and your life will feel less meaningful.

If we are certain of our purposes, then hard work isn't a problem. Writing our novel can make us feel sad and ill, so poorly is it going and so much work does it require. Yet our genes may well be singing and dancing, profoundly happy knowing that we are living one of our life purposes. When you doubt that writing your novel matters, say to yourself,

"It matters on the genetic level, and I want to make my genes happy!" Who knows if this is literally true? It just might be.

Your genes want you to live with purpose. They want to be "happy" in precisely that way, and you will stay healthier when you live in alignment with your life purposes and, as a result of those efforts, create meaning. Because it is all too easy to doubt our own decisions and life purposes, we regularly pester ourselves about whether what we are attempting is really meaningful, really matters, or really is one of our life purposes. When we do this, we enter an existential dark night of doubt, and then our genes are much less happy. Some sort of sickness is likely coming, such as despair, cravings, or a physical illness.

What must you do when you experience such doubt? You must reinitiate that most basic of conversations, the one where you chat with yourself about your values, principles, and life-purpose choices. If you come around again to believing in your current choice, then you must announce that you intend to make yourself proud through your efforts in the service of that choice. You stand up again. This gesture will make your genes instantly happy! And if you can't come around to believing in your choice, then you must make a strong new choice. That, too, will please your genes.

Hardly anything is more important than recognizing the connection between living your life purposes and your emotional and physical health. It is physically good for us to live our life purposes. We may one day learn that there is a clear and strict relationship between life purpose and genetic happiness. For now, it is wise to presume that such a relationship exists. Do not chase happiness; live your life purposes instead. That will likely produce the deepest happiness possible!

Jenny's Necessary Things

Jenny found herself trapped in the sort of acquisitive and materialistic family we've been discussing. Everyone in the family seemed obsessed with not only knowing about but also owning the newest and latest things: the latest smartphone, the latest coffeemaker, the latest off-road vehicle, the latest smart toilet, the latest designer handbag, the latest watch able to tell time to a depth of twenty thousand feet.

Her father complained constantly that their three-car garage was simply not large enough for their many cars and their many sporting toys — snowboards, Jet Skis, bicycles, and more. He threatened almost daily to move them to a house with a four- or five-car garage. Her mother pored over home-design magazines, coveting some new look or other and moaning about how outdated their kitchen and their many bathrooms were.

Jenny knew that there were worse problems than having a family that endlessly talked about things, craved things, and bought things. Yet she experienced the constant attention her family lavished on things as a form of low-grade torture. As so often happens in such cases, Jenny's response was to contemplate repudiating all things. She began to obsess about an austere life completely free of things: she could see herself with a cot, a teacup, and a vase for flowers.

We talked about this. I wondered if there was a different, less austere and less radical way to go. I asked her whether, if she discerned that her life purposes necessitated owning certain things, she could be comfortable with those things. What if she wanted to be a doctor? Would she scorn the latest medical devices just because they were "things"? Finally she agreed that she would not. I asked her to create a list of her life-purpose choices and then to identify material things that logically and maybe necessarily went with those choices.

The next time we chatted, she began by laughing. "That exercise was actually an eye-opener!" she said.

> For almost everything on my life-purpose choice list, there were things that I would need in order to actually live those choices! I can't be the biochemist I want to be without lab equipment. I can't have children and not need diapers and bottles and at least all the basics! I can't...I can't travel without a suitcase! So I came to the following conclusions. I'm not going to roll my eyes at what my parents buy — I am going to try to let that all go. For myself, I am going to continue not to care about newness, not to care about brand names and designer labels, and not suppose that because something is more expensive than something else it's better. But I am not going to wage a war with things. I am going to be an ascetic who is easy with things!

If you object to materialism, brand consciousness, and the acquisitive mindset, you may find yourself wanting to go in the opposite direction, toward a renunciation of material things and a radically ascetic lifestyle. Don't go completely overboard! Things are not the enemy, and acquiring and owning things are not sins. You do not have to renounce all material goods in order to protest your family's acquisitive and materialistic ways. It is really fine if you want something or need something: it doesn't mean that you have succumbed to or been infected by your family's philosophy!

Just as the child of an alcoholic might naturally make the

decision to never drink a drop of alcohol, you might make the decision to own nothing. But that is an extreme position that will end up depriving you of useful and beautiful things as well. Choose as your mantra something more like "Things aren't the enemy," "I can have some things," "Wanting something doesn't make me spoiled," or another mantra that captures the idea that while you are being watchful about owning too many things, you will not go all the way over to the far side of hating things and treating them as the enemy.

Tackling the Boredom behind All That Acquisitiveness

Busy people who are rushing around making money so as to acquire things may still be, for all that busyness and for all the toys that they acquire to keep themselves amused, deeply bored. Indeed, the running and the buying may be the ways that they keep from noticing how deeply bored they are.

Chronic boredom is a huge threat to your mental health because of what it signifies: uncertainty about meaning and your life purposes. Mild boredom or occasional boredom is little more than clouds briefly passing across the sun. But chronic boredom is a very different matter. Because it feels so unpleasant in its own right and because we know that it signals an ongoing meaning crisis that can lead to sadness and despair, it frightens us. The mere whiff of it causes us to rush off and do something. This accounts for so much of our busyness and acquisitiveness: we are trying to outrun our boredom and the meaning crisis it signals.

What we rush off to do may be completely unworthy of us. We fear boredom, we rush away when we smell it, and our effort to escape it may prove as much a misadventure as a time waster and a money waster.

Actively make meaning, and you will fear boredom less. Live your life purposes on a daily basis, and you will fear boredom less. Educate yourself about what "making meaning" entails (see my book *Life Purpose Boot Camp* for more on this undertaking) and do the important work of identifying and articulating your life purposes so that you can go about living them. This will improve your mental health dramatically! Here are some tips:

- *Create a small ceremony that helps you remember that boredom is not something to fear.* Boredom is a mere psychological state that, like any psychological state, will move on. Since you can train yourself to deal with boredom by making meaning and by living your life purposes, there isn't very much to fear. You don't have to run away at the mere whiff of it!

- *Treat boredom as the transitory state it is and not as an indictment of life itself.* Don't leap from "I'm bored" to "Life has nothing to offer me." Boredom will pass. You might even ceremonially reframe a little boredom as a good thing and as a prelude to useful activity. Whether you "need" boredom or not, at least fear it less!

- *Do a little investigating.* Is the boredom masking some other feeling like anger, resentment, or rage? Often boredom is the "safe" feeling that we learn to tolerate so as not to have to deal with a darker feeling underneath. Is something painful going on underneath the boredom that you ought to know about?

CEREMONY: Inquiring about Your Boredom

Boredom is very often a symptom of meaning problems. If boredom is a problem for you, ask yourself, "What is my boredom about?"

You may discover that it is masking some anger or resentment. You may find instead that you have simply developed the bad habit of saying, "I'm bored!" at the least loss of interest and enthusiasm. Or you may discover that it is indeed a symptom of meaning problems and that it is in your best interests to learn more about the art and practice of making meaning.

Engage in this simple ceremony today, and maybe you'll learn what your boredom wants to tell you.

Much of our rushing — around town, around cyberspace, and inside our own mind — and much of our acquisitive nature and materialistic obsessions are caused by our desire to ward off boredom and evade the meaning problems that boredom signals. We would fear boredom much less if we were effectively dealing with those meaning problems. Deal with those, and your boredom, your frantic busyness, and your acquisitiveness will dramatically decrease.

Food for Thought

1. To what extent was your family of origin an acquisitive or materialistic family?
2. If your family of origin was an acquisitive or materialistic family, what were the consequences for you?

3. To what extent is your current family an acquisitive or materialistic family?
4. If you currently inhabit an acquisitive or materialistic family, how can you use your tool kit to deal more effectively with the challenges you're facing?

CHAPTER EIGHTEEN

Frustrated, Hopeless, and Defeated Families

Everyone is frustrated sometimes. But some people — and some families — experience life as painfully and persistently frustrating. Maybe they feel that they can never get ahead financially. Maybe they're dogged by accidents, illnesses, and bad luck. Maybe their various careers have hit dead ends. Maybe their dreams have failed to materialize. This last situation creates some of the most pernicious, deep-seated frustrations, which invariably affect everyone in the family.

Picture a family in which some or even all of the members of the family feel that their dreams — to be a painter, to be a musician, to get out of an office cubicle and be their own boss, to move up in social or economic class, or to get out of their claustrophobic town — have little or no chance of ever coming true. They may feel doubly frustrated if they experience their potential as unrealized, either because they have failed themselves or were prevented from making full use of their talents and abilities.

These are often among the most painful families in which to grow up. Sadness runs deep; fights erupt over nothing; family members do impulsive things like quitting the job they hate on the spur of the moment or abruptly leaving home to "find themselves" or to "start fresh." In families keeping secrets of this sort — that the family's dreams were never realized and the family's potential never manifested — everyone walks on eggshells, knowing not to broach certain subjects without quite knowing why.

Even someone who is successful may feel severely frustrated. Success does not inoculate us against frustration. No writer was ever more successful during his lifetime than the Russian author Leo Tolstoy, yet he felt intensely frustrated by his inability to maintain meaning in his life. Nothing, not even the prospect of yet more fame, felt meaningful to him, and so, in very old age, he ran away from home and died at a railway station in full flight from his privileged, successful, and nevertheless frustrating life.

Judy's Need for Clarity

My client Judy had married a man who had always wanted to be a rock musician but who had become a successful lawyer instead. Judy presumed that over time, the many good things in his life — his children, his well-paying job, his relationship with her — would allow him to heal and either put his dream behind him or to find some way to enjoy playing as an amateur musician. That healing never happened. If anything, he grew relentlessly sourer and more disenchanted with his life, taking out his frustrations on his employees, his children, and Judy.

She felt genuinely confounded, because she believed her husband had so many good things going in his life. Why weren't those things enough? How could the dream of being a rock musician continue to matter now that he was in his late thirties? It simply made no sense to her. And he didn't even seem to like music any longer! He'd go months on end without listening to music of any sort. Then every so often he'd buy some lavish piece of equipment and claim that he was creating a home recording studio. He'd use the equipment once or twice and never touch it again. What was going on?

I asked her to think about the eight skills. Which of them did she need to manifest in order to improve her situation? Almost without hesitation, she said, "I need to be clear."

"Clear about what?"

"Clear about what is actually going on, not what I wish was going on or what I think should be going on. What I think *should* be going on is that he should get over it already! I need to get clear about what is actually going on, the extent to which his frustration and unhappiness really play themselves out day in and day out — and whether that's too much for me to take."

"How will you gain this clarity?"

"It feels silly to say it, but I think I'll keep some kind of notebook. I need to get clear on when he's mean to the kids, when he's mean to me, when he gets moody and unavailable, when he wants to bite everyone's head off. I need to make sure that I'm not making up how bad it all feels or how often it happens. In a way I want to give him the benefit of the doubt — maybe, just maybe, I'm exaggerating. But I need to know one way or the other."

The upshot of her gaining clarity, a process that took several months, was a messy but necessary divorce. She didn't really believe that his failed musician's dream was the real cause of his frustration, but whatever the real cause — which she thought might have something to do with his relationship with his powerful, extraordinarily successful father — the sourness, surliness, and unhappiness were real enough. And she didn't want to live with them. When she took the radical but necessary step of divorcing him, his frustrations became a thing of her past and not her everyday present.

Mira and Mark

Another client, Mira, grew up with a father who painted every spare minute that he wasn't running his dry-cleaning business and a mother who swooned over her husband's talent and output. His paintings, traditional religious scenes done in broken glass, ceramic tile shards, and sand he collected from the desert, were bizarre, dramatic, and perhaps even wonderful; but he made no effort to sell them, and he exclaimed all the time, "They'll discover me, or the hell with them!" He himself never seemed frustrated by the fact that he sold nothing; but his wife was frustrated enough for the both of them.

She complained bitterly to Mira that someone — Mira took it to mean her — should get her father's work better known. Neither she nor her mother knew what that entailed or what steps they ought to take; nor did either one of them seem inclined to research the market and figure out how to proceed. Instead, a certain dynamic persisted: her father thumbed his nose at the established ways of selling art through galleries, her mother complained to Mira all the time that he wasn't recognized, and Mira fell right into line, brimming over with guilt.

This dynamic continued long after both her father and her mother passed away. Saddled with his huge output and paralyzed as to how to sell paintings, Mira remained the dutiful, guilt-ridden, frustrated daughter.

A third client, Mark, was sexually frustrated. He explained that he had a high sex drive, and his wife had a low sex drive. In the beginning, he presumed that they would meet somewhere in the middle, that they would arrive at some sort of reasonable accommodation that he could live with. From the start, he doubted that he would ever really be satisfied with that sort of compromise; but he had no inkling of how miserable the "sex thing" would become. It was now almost the only thing he thought about: how much he resented his wife's withholding and how sad he felt not to be loved, touched, or wanted.

He was tired of being rebuffed, tired of begging, tired of the whole thing. He didn't want "substitute" answers like affairs, pornography, or more masturbation. He wanted to be with someone who wanted sex, who desired him, and who enjoyed physical contact. That wasn't his wife — or at least didn't appear to be. Resigned and pessimistic, he couldn't picture a solution.

Our despair grows when, in addition to our suffering, we suffer from a lack of possible answers. Mark decided to try a round of cognitive behavioral therapy, to see if he could learn to feel better even if nothing changed but his own attitude. Later I learned that Mark had divorced; his wife had left him.

My Wife Has the Problem

What does frustration sound like from the other side, from the side of the person causing the frustration? Listen in to a coaching session with Jake, a filmmaker in his early thirties, whose own frustrations were causing his wife all sorts of frustrations.

"How are you doing?" I asked.

"I'm good. I'm pushing along with my film — it's getting there. It's my wife...she has the problem."

"What's that?"

"The film is going to cost…a lot. And we're spending our own money on it. The money we'd saved as a down payment for a house."

"She isn't on board with that idea?"

"She hates it. We've had hellacious fights."

"I don't think I'd be too happy either!" I laughed. "But you seem to have made up your mind. About the film versus your relationship."

"No! It isn't like that at all —"

"You're not holding the film as more important than the relationship?"

"No!" he said excitedly. "If she could just see where this will lead…how good this will be for both of us."

I nodded. "You want her to change her mind and get on board with an open heart?"

"Yes!"

"While you're spending the down payment for the house she wants."

He bit his lip.

"Did she save that money?" I said.

He didn't reply. "Part of it came from a small inheritance I got!" he finally blurted out. "This film could win an Academy Award!"

"You've tried to find outside funding?" I said.

He shook his head. "That's way too hard! We have the money, and we have credit cards, and I can borrow more from my parents if need be. I can keep it all right inside our family and get the film done without having to go around begging."

"Begging?"

He made a face. "That's what it feels like!"

"You've tried it?"

"No." He hesitated. "I wouldn't even know where to begin."

"So it seems easier to spend the down payment money than investigate funding?"

"I don't feel like you're really on my side," he said, shifting uneasily.

"Why? Because I think your wife's concerns also matter?"

He got up abruptly and walked around the room. Finally he sat back down.

"I don't think you understand the upside of this project. Everybody I tell about the concept loves it."

"So tell me," I said. "How much of the movie is made?"

"I have a rough draft of the script. A rough draft of most of the script — half at least."

I nodded. "But you've already spent a lot of money?"

"On equipment. You need the right equipment. And I paid to have an original score composed — that's been a mess! And I hired someone to scout locations.... There are a lot of expenses before you can actually get started!"

I nodded. "Absolutely. But I'm trying to understand your approach to this. Why commission an original score when money is tight?"

He threw up his hands. "I could hear just the right music in my head. But the composer I hired didn't really get it."

I took a breath.

"Okay," I said. "Let me make sure I'm getting this right. Are you saying that you're having problems making this movie, or are you just having problems getting your wife's buy-in?"

He shook his head. "Well, it's very complicated making a movie, and this is my first one. And I got off on the wrong foot with the composer and with this editor I hired to look at my partial script…and I was supposed to get better tech support on the equipment I bought, that's been kind of a nightmare… but I just wish my wife was in this with me. She keeps nagging me, and I can't concentrate on getting the script finished."

"A lot of relationship problems," I said.

He shrugged. "I just need people to do what they say. That's all."

"Your wife said that she would support you in this?"

"She did! In the beginning. I told her about my dream when we first met, and she was all gung ho for it. Then some years passed while I was working on the script…and she changed her tune. She was all for it in the beginning!"

"Things changed."

"My dream didn't!"

We continued in this vein. I renewed my wondering about the possibility and reasonableness of finding outside funding. Jake wasn't interested. I wondered if it made sense not to spend more money until he had a viable script ready. That wasn't possible. I wondered if there was any way his wife could get her house, and he could get his film. No. I asked whether he had entered into clear agreements with the composer, the location scout, the editor, the tech support people — of course he had. Everything was fine, if only his wife would support him.

Some of the silences grew very long. He had less and less to say — he knew I was thinking that he was the one with the problem. He couldn't wait to leave. Finally our time was up, and he got his wish. We didn't set up a second appointment.

If you grew up or are currently living in a family seething with frustrations, where family members failed to realize their dreams and felt defeated, remember that the past does not predict the future. The failed dreams and unrealized potential of family members do not doom you to the same fate. You must understand and live this truth in a fundamental way. The mere intellectual understanding that you still have a chance won't suffice to free you from your unfortunate legacy. Just saying, "That won't happen to me!" or "I won't let that happen to me!" isn't enough. You need to employ every tool in your tool kit to keep hope alive, to relieve your frustrations, and to stand undefeated.

The following ceremony can help.

CEREMONY: Giving Life a Hearty Thumbs-Up

Over time, people's frustrations, broken dreams, disappointments, and significant setbacks can cause them to feel cheated. After too many failures — and without quite knowing that it has happened — people give up on life. They continue to go through the motions, and they may even experience occasional happiness. But at heart they feel thwarted that life has turned out to be such a paltry thing. They make an unconscious evaluation that life has cheated them.

You might evaluate life harshly for any or all of the reasons we've been discussing. Maybe it's because you went unloved as a child. Maybe because you must spend a stupendous amount of your time just earning a living. Maybe because you see immorality rewarded and good deeds punished. Maybe because you haven't had a single one of your dreams come true. Maybe just because you expected *more* from life, from others, and from yourself.

As true as it may feel, this evaluation harms you. It

contributes to everything from so-called clinical depression to addiction. If you have come to hate life, how can you also love life? This negative evaluation kills love and hope for the future.

If you've decided that nothing in life can ever feel genuinely enjoyable, then you will instantly sour experiences that you might otherwise experience as joyful. If you've made this unconscious evaluation, now is the time to change your mind — and your heart. You must, for the sake of experiencing life as meaningful and for the sake of your mental health, evaluate it more generously.

This doesn't mean that you need to paste on a smiley face or settle for less than you want and need. But it does mean that you need to change your conception of life. Rather than considering life a fraud and a cheat, what sort of picture can you paint that allows you to view it more positively? Might it work to hold life as a project, as an opportunity to live your life purposes, as a responsibility, or as an adventure?

A simple strategy to employ to help you feel more charitable and compassionate toward life is to give it a hearty thumbs-up — literally. Try making that gesture several times today. Have a conversation with yourself about what thoughts and feelings arise in you when you do it. Your goal is to find a deep willingness to evaluate life more positively. Your thumbs-up gesture is your physical representation of that effort. Give that gesture a try today.

Food for Thought

1. To what extent was your family of origin a frustrated, hopeless, or defeated family?
2. If your family of origin was a frustrated, hopeless, or defeated family, what were the consequences for you?
3. To what extent is your current family a frustrated, hopeless, or defeated family?
4. If you currently inhabit a frustrated, hopeless, or defeated family, how can you use your tool kit to deal more effectively with the challenges you're facing?

Twelve Tips for Emotional and Mental Health

Growing up in a difficult family or living in a difficult family inevitably produces negative consequences of all sorts. These are on top of the other challenges you face — challenges around life purpose and meaning, making a living and paying the bills, getting ill, falling out of love, making mistakes and disappointing yourself, and more.

I hope the tool kit of skills I've described will help you navigate all this difficulty a little better. Here are another twelve tips that may also prove valuable. Some underline issues I've discussed already, and others add to the discussion. I hope that they serve you!

1. Accept Being Human

Human beings experience emotional distress in all sorts of ways: as sadness, anxiety, addictions, unproductive obsessions, unwanted compulsions, repetitive self-sabotaging behaviors, physical ailments, conflicts of conscience, despair, boredom, and angry, bleak, and agitated moods. Can you accept this? When distress returns, can you stand unsurprised and, instead of blaming the universe, shrinking from the moment, or throwing up your hands, say, "I am a human being. I am nothing but human! Now, let me do what I can to gather myself and make myself proud."

2. Acknowledge the Constraints of Personality

Our personality is at once a pressure cooker and a windowless room. It sends our mind racing, it builds up grievances, it chooses sides, it frightens itself, it experiences disappointment and loss, it maintains dark secrets, it gets violently aggrieved, it wants what it wants, and it knows how to hate at least as well as it knows how to love. Yet what it does and how it operates seem not to interest its owner. It is as if we are born with one genetic instruction before all others: "Never look in the mirror!" Your personality is your responsibility, and your personality is your destiny. Only you can improve it.

3. Be Yourself

You must improve yourself — but you must also be yourself. This means asking for what you want, setting boundaries, having your own beliefs and opinions, standing up for your values, wearing the clothes you want to wear, eating the food you want to eat, saying the things you want to say, and in countless other ways being you and not somebody small or false. This doesn't mean denying the importance of others — of individuals, communities, or civil society. Rather, it means that if you are gay, you are gay; if you are smart, you are smart; if you require freedom, you demand freedom. Make use of your available personality to upgrade your formed personality.

4. Invent Yourself

You come with attributes, capacities, and proclivities, and you are molded in a certain environment. Your personality forms, and you tend to repeat behaviors that don't serve you. But at some point you must say, "Okay, whatever is original to me — whether it's an extra dose of sadness, a bit too much sensitivity, or something else — and however I've been formed — to shrink, to fantasize, something else — now *who do I want to be?*" You reduce your emotional distress by deciding to become a person who will experience less emotional distress: a calmer person, a less critical person, a less egoistic person, a more productive person, or a less self-abusive person. You make the clear, conscious decision that, no matter how tightly wound you may be, you will make use of your available personality and your remaining freedom in the service of your life-purpose choices and your other important intentions.

5. Love and Be Loved

Part of our nature requires solitude and a substantial rugged individualism. But this isn't the whole of our nature. We feel happier, warmer, and just much better, we live longer, and we experience life as more meaningful if we love and let ourselves be loved. We must be individuals, but we must also relate to other people. To do both requires that we acknowledge the reality of others, that we not only speak but also listen, and that we make ourselves fit for relationships by eliminating our worst faults and growing up. If you withhold, if you lead with criticism, if you can't get over yourself — whatever you do that harms your chances at love, make remedying that one of your primary life purposes.

6. Get a Grip on Your Mind

Nothing causes more emotional distress than the thoughts we think. We must work at identifying the thoughts that don't serve us, disputing them and demanding that they go away, and substituting more useful thoughts. Only you can get a grip on your own mind: if you won't do that work, you will live in distress. Do you think you are ruined? That thought will ruin you. Think you are unworthy? That thought will diminish you. Think the world is a cheat? That thought will disempower you. Your distress is not only held firmly in place by the thoughts that you think, but it also *is* those thoughts.

Imagine a day without inner commentary about everything that is hard, everything that is scary, and everything that is wrong. Wouldn't that be a better day?

7. Heal the Past

We are not so completely in control of our mind, our emotions, or our being that we can always prevent old sore points and the residue of trauma from returning with a vengeance. They have a way of pestering us as anxious sweats, nightmares, sudden sadness, and waves of anger or defeat. They remain not only as memory but as personality as well, woven into our fabric. But we can nevertheless try to heal the past by thinking through how we want to relate to these deep memories. What will you do when you are struck by a flashback? What tactics will you employ when you well up with rage or regret? From what reserve will you call up the energy to move through the pain? Healing is not a metaphor: it is a call to action.

8. Flip Off the Anxiety Switch

Anxiety can ruin our equilibrium, darken our mood, and make all the challenging tasks of living that much harder. There are many anxiety management strategies you might want to try — including breathing techniques, cognitive techniques, and relaxation techniques — but the most effective thing you can do is locate that inner switch that controls your anxious nature and flip it to the "off" position. With that one gesture you announce that you will no longer overdramatize, no longer catastrophize, no longer live a fearful life or create unnecessary anxiety for yourself. Anxiety is part of our warning system against danger. By flipping the switch inside you that controls it, you declare that you will not live under siege and under threat. Threats will remain and return, but flooding the chemicals of anxiety through your system is not a helpful way to meet those threats. Being calm is better.

9. Make Meaning

It's important that we realize that meaning is a psychological experience and that by identifying and adopting strong life purposes we help ourselves create those psychological experiences, causing life to feel meaningful. We have probably never thought through our personal requirements for determining meaning. We can have much more meaning in our life if we stop looking for it, as if it were lost or as if someone else knew more about it than we did, and realize that it is in our power to determine meaning for ourselves. By making daily meaning investments and by seizing daily meaning opportunities, we hold meaning crises at bay and experience life as meaningful. Meaning problems produce severe emotional distress, and learning the art of making meaning, according to our values, dramatically reduces that distress.

10. Focus on Life Purpose and Meaning and Not on Mood

You can decide that the meaning you hope to make and the life purposes you intend to manifest are more important to you than the mood you happen to find yourself in. Rather than saying, "I'm blue today," you say, "I have my business to build," "I have my novel to write," or "I have my personality to upgrade." You start each day by announcing to yourself exactly how you intend to make meaning on that day, how you intend to deal with your routine chores and tasks, how you intend to relax — how, in short, you mean to spend your day — and you consider all of that, the rich and the mundane alike, as the project of your life, one that you are living with grace and in good spirits. You reduce your emotional distress by focusing more on your intentions and less on your mood.

11. Upgrade Your Personality

You may not yet be the person you would like to be or the person you need to be in order to reduce your emotional distress. You may be angrier than you would like to be, more impulsive, more scattered, more self-sabotaging, more undisciplined, more frightened. If so, you require a personality upgrade, which of course only you can undertake. You embark on this upgrade by choosing a feature of your personality that you would like to upgrade and then asking yourself, "What sorts of thoughts and what sorts of actions align with this upgrade intention?" Then you think the appropriate thoughts and take the necessary action. In this way you become the person you would like to be, someone actually capable of reducing your emotional distress.

12. Deal with Your Circumstances

Would you experience more distress relaxing at the beach or enduring a long jail sentence? Would you experience more distress if you hated going to work or loved going to work? Our circumstances matter to us: our economic circumstances, our relationships, our work conditions, our health, whether our nation is at peace or occupied by invaders. Many circumstances are completely out of our control, but many are within our control. We can change jobs or careers, we can divorce, we can reduce our calorie intake, we can choose to stand up or keep quiet. As a result of these improvements, we will likely feel emotionally better. Reducing our emotional distress requires taking real action in the real world.

Emotional health and pain-free living are not the same things. You can be as emotionally healthy as a person can be and still reel from the pain of losing a loved one, judging your occupation meaningless, or finding your intimate relationship falling apart. You can still have real troubles every single day accepting your mortality, dealing with your lack of income, or tolerating your chronic pain. We must not judge emotional health by the amount of pain a person experiences. A moral, mental, and emotional giant may still be plagued by sadness.

What is emotional health, then, if it isn't the absence of pain? It is a kind of vibrant wisdom, a dynamic executive awareness coupled with a powerful resistance to humbug with a bit of philosophical wryness thrown in, a vibrant wisdom where you acknowledge your human nature and the facts of existence, see your life as your loving and deserving project, and live according to your life purposes, making meaning according to your values. You are completely in the fray and just enough above the fray to see what it is all about. Does pain still come? Of course it does. You haven't learned how to walk on water — what you have learned is how to walk on fire. This wisdom will help you — and it will help your family too!

I hope that this book has served you a little. Good luck to you.

Notes

p. 79   *Every individual and family experience two types of "anxiety":*
Steven M. Harris and Dean M. Busby, "Pant-Legs and Pathology:
The Marriage of Individual and Family Assessment," *Contemporary
Family Therapy* 19, no. 4 (1997): 507, doi:10.1023/A:1026131004821.

p. 90   *From 33–75% of men to 26–70% of women have been involved
in an extramarital relationship:* M.M. Jeanfreau, A.P. Jurich, and
M.D. Mong, "Risk Factors Associated with Women's Marital
Infidelity," *Contemporary Family Therapy* 36, no. 3 (2014): 327,
doi:10.1007/s10591-014-9309-3.

p. 94   *Compassionate love appeared to help mothers:* J.G. Miller, S.
Kahle, M. Lopez, and P.D. Hastings, "Compassionate Love Buffers
Stress-Reactive Mothers from Fight-or-Flight Parenting," *Develop-
mental Psychology* 51, no. 1 (January 2015): 36–43, doi:10.1037
/a0038236.

p. 102   *Children whose parents divorce are more likely to see their own
marriages end in divorce:* Brandt C. Gardner, Dean M. Busby,
Brandon K. Burr, and Sarah E. Lyon, "Getting to the Root of Relationship Attributions: Family of Origin Perspectives on Self and
Partner Views," *Contemporary Family Therapy* 33, no. 3 (September
2011): 253–72, doi:10.1007/s10591-011-9163-5.

p. 102   *Children, particularly daughters, provide much of the family care:* Twyla J. Hill, *Family Caregiving in Aging Populations* (Basingstoke, UK: Palgrave Pivot, 2015): 40.

p. 103　*Rivalry, competition and anxiety about your place in your parents' affections:* Jeanne Safer, *Cain's Legacy: Liberating Siblings from a Lifetime of Rage, Shame, Secrecy, and Regret* (New York: Basic Books, 2012): 3.

p. 104　*Although the amount of sibling contact diminishes as children age:* R. J. Waldinger, G. E. Vaillant, and E. J. Orav, "Childhood Sibling Relationships as a Predictor of Major Depression in Adulthood: A 30-Year Prospective Study," *American Journal of Psychiatry* 164, no. 6 (June 2007): 949–54.

p. 105　*The provision of care for a parent usually falls on the shoulders of one offspring:* S. D. Whiteman, S. M. McHale, and A. Soli, "Theoretical Perspectives on Sibling Relationships," *Journal of Family Theory and Review* 3 (2011): 124–39, doi:10.1111/j.1756-2589.2011 .00087.

p. 114　*One important key to understanding child-to-parent abuse:* Eric A. Maisel, "Laurie Reid on Child-to-Parent Violence," *Rethinking Mental Health* (blog), *Psychology Today*, March 11, 2016, https://www.psychologytoday.com/blog/rethinking-mental -health/201603/laurie-reid-child-parent-violence.

p. 115　*Don't ignore sibling aggression:* Sherri Gordon, "Eight Ways to Avoid Raising a Bully," Verywell.com, August 31, 2016, https://www .verywell.com/avoid-raising-a-bully-460515.

p. 117　*While previous research has identified avoidance as a coping strategy:* Dina M. Carbonell, Helen Z. Reinherz, and William R. Beardslee, "Adaptation and Coping in Childhood and Adolescence for Those at Risk for Depression in Emerging Adulthood," *Child and Adolescent Social Work Journal* 22, no. 5 (December 2005): 395–416.

p. 119　*It may not be fair, but it's important to be real:* Marie Hartwell-Walker, "Teens: Coping with Being Unwanted, Unloved and Unhappy," PsychCentral, http://psychcentral.com/lib/teens-coping -with-being-unwanted-unloved-and-unhappy, accessed January 11, 2017.

p. 124　*I failed birth:* "Falling Short: Seven Writers Reflect on Failure," *Guardian*, June 22, 2013, www.theguardian.com/books/2013/jun/22 /falling-short-writers-reflect-failure.

p. 136　*Despite the fact that workaholism has been cited as the best-dressed family problem:* Bryan A. Robinson, "Workaholism and

Family Functioning: A Profile of Familial Relationships, Psychological Outcomes, and Research Considerations," *Contemporary Family Therapy* 23, no. 1 (2001): 123–35.

p. 149   *Dysfunctional rules hinder communication:* J. H. Larson, M. Taggart-Reedy, and S. M. Wilson, "The Effects of Perceived Dysfunctional Family of Origin Rules on the Dating Relationships of Young Adults," *Contemporary Family Therapy* 23, no. 4 (2001) 23: 489, doi:10.1023/A:1013009213860.

p. 153   *Research has shown that children of authoritarian families are more prone to suffering from low self-esteem:* "The Essence of the Strict Authoritarian Parenting Style and the Long Term Effects," Positive Parenting Ally, www.positive-parenting-ally.com /authoritarian-parenting.html, accessed January 11, 2017.

p. 155   *Authoritarianism is something authoritarian followers and authoritarian leaders cook up between themselves:* Bob Altemeyer, *The Authoritarians* (2006), 8. Available at http://members.shaw.ca /jeanaltemeyer/drbob/TheAuthoritarians.pdf, accessed December 10, 2016.

p. 156   *We found that children whose parents use more authoritarian- type parenting strategies tend to develop more aggression:* Stephen Smith, "Children of 'Tiger Parents' Develop More Aggression and Depression, Research Shows," *CBS News*, June 20, 2013, www .cbsnews.com/news/children-of-tiger-parents-develop-more -aggression-and-depression-research-shows.

p. 160   *The goal is to change and transform the behavior:* Carl Sayles, "Transformation Change — Based on the Model of Virginia Satir," *Contemporary Family Therapy* 24, no. 1 (March 2002): 93–109.

p. 173   *Once our basic material needs are satisfied, our level of income makes little difference:* Steve Taylor, "The Madness of Materialism," *Psychology Today*, March 10, 2012, www.psychologytoday.com/blog /out-the-darkness/201203/the-madness-materialism.

p. 173   *Children who are more materialistic are less happy:* Campaign for a Commercial-Free Childhood, "Materialistic Values and Family Stress," www.commercialfreechildhood.org/issue /materialistic-values-and-family-stress, accessed January 11, 2017.

p. 175   *The researchers assessed and took blood samples from 80 healthy adults:* Melissa Breyer, "Different Kinds of Happiness Affect Genes in Different Ways, Study Finds," Mother Nature Network, August 2, 2013, www.mnn.com/health/fitness-well-being/stories/different -kinds-of-happiness-affect-genes-in-different-ways-study.

Index

About the Author

Eric Maisel, PhD, is the author of more than fifty books, among them *The Future of Mental Health, Rethinking Depression, Life Purpose Boot Camp, The Van Gogh Blues, Mastering Creative Anxiety, Why Smart People Hurt,* and *Coaching the Artist Within.*

A retired family therapist and active coach and mental health advocate in the areas of critical psychology and critical psychiatry, Dr. Maisel writes the "Rethinking Mental Health" blog for *Psychology Today* and the "Coaching the Artist Within" print column for *Professional Artist* magazine. His latest book is *Humanizing the Helping Professions* (Routledge, forthcoming 2018).

Dr. Maisel lectures nationally and internationally. He facilitates deep writing workshops in locations like San Francisco, New York, London, Paris, and Rome and at workshop centers like the Esalen Institute, the Omega Institute, and the Kripalu Yoga Center. He presents keynote addresses for organizations like the International Society for Ethical Psychology and Psychiatry and the International Association of Pastel Societies.

You can learn more about Dr. Maisel's workshops, trainings, and services at www.ericmaisel.com; about his classes and guides at www.ericmaiselsolutions.com; and about his mental health advocacy at www.thefutureofmentalhealth.com. You can contact Dr. Maisel at ericmaisel@hotmail.com.